Multilateral Investment Insurance and Private Investment in the Third World

Multilateral Investment Insurance and Private Investment in the Third World

MANFRED HOLTHUS
DIETRICH KEBSCHULL
KARL WOLFGANG MENCK

Routledge
Taylor & Francis Group

LONDON AND NEW YORK

First published 1987 by Transaction Publishers
Edition 1987

Published 2019 by Routledge
2 Park Square, Milton Park, Abingdon, Oxon OX14 4RN
52 Vanderbilt Avenue, New York, NY 10017

Routledge is an imprint of the Taylor & Francis Group, an informa business

Copyright © 1987 by Taylor & Francis

Library of Congress Catalog Number: 85-16394

Library of Congress Cataloging in Publication Data

Holthus, Manfred.
    Multilateral investment insurance and private investment in the Third World.

    Reprint. Originally published: Hamburg: Verlag Weltarchiv, 1984.
    Bibliography: p.
    1. Insurance, Investment guaranty.   2. Insurance, Investment guaranty—Developing countries.
I. Kebschull, Dietrich.   II. Menck, Karl Wolfgang.
III. Title
HG4538.H34   1985   368.8′53′0091724   85-16394
ISBN 0-88738-615-6 (pbk.)

ISBN 13: 978-0-88738-615-2 (pbk)
ISBN 13: 978-1-138-52847-5 (hbk)

PREFACE

Developments in the world economy in recent years have been such that the flow of capital to the countries of the Third World has been less than expected for realising their growth objectives. As a consequence, efforts have been redoubled everywhere to attract capital in the form of direct investment, which has sometimes provoked strong criticism. In this connection the establishment of a multilateral guarantee scheme to reduce the risks associated with overseas investment is again under discussion. A new proposal for the design of such a scheme was put forward in 1982 by the World Bank.

The HWWA has long concerned itself with the questions of direct investment in developing countries and the promotion of such investment. It therefore gladly accepted a commission from the Federal Ministry for Economic Affairs to analyse and comment upon the necessity and suitability of the World Bank proposal. The study was concluded in May 1983. The World Bank Staff Studies on the same subject that were completed shortly after that date could therefore not be taken into consideration; nonetheless, they arrive at no conclusions that would occasion a change in the opinions expressed here.

The study is a contribution to the continuing economic discussion. As the proposal under consideration has not been worked out in every detail, a number of assumptions had to be made which will very probably hold true if the multilateral guarantee scheme were implemented; if the configuration of the scheme were fundamentally different, however, the conclusions would have to be reviewed.

The authors are members of the Department on Developing Countries and North-South Economic Relations of the HWWA. They wish to thank in particular Dr. Beckmann, Mr. Rösler and Dr. Wurmstich of Treuarbeit Aktiengesellschaft in Hamburg for their valuable suggestions and support with carrying out the study. Especial thanks are also due to Dr. Burkhardt of the Federal Ministry for Economic Affairs and the representatives of the other government departments involved for their constructive criticisms. Nonetheless, the authors are responsible for the content of the study.

Hamburg, September 1983   Dietrich Kebschull

TABLE OF CONTENTS

INTRODUCTION

The study is concerned with the plans to introduce a multi-lateral investment guarantee scheme. Proposals of this type are not new. They were discussed intensively at the end of the fifties but declined in importance in later years, not least because of the rapid creation of overseas investment guarantee institutions at national level. More recently, however, increased attention has again been paid to proposals for the establishment of a multilateral agency. This is particularly true of the World Bank proposal, which is the central topic of this study. The proposal itself was unveiled last year. Its authors imply that the trend in underlying economic conditions in recent years clearly favours the introduction of a multilateral scheme and that the expansion of the private-sector component within overall economic co-operation with Third World countries calls for such an arrangement. In keeping with most proposals for multilateral schemes, the World Bank plan sets out from the premisses that

- additional foreign investment capital for developing countries could be mobilised on a large scale if the investment risks were reduced by means of a multilateral guarantee scheme;

- existing national insurance schemes display a series of shortcomings that could be avoided in a multilateral system.

In order to assess the potential and limits of the proposed scheme from the economic point of view it is necessary to test the soundness of these premisses before examining questions that would arise upon implementation of a multilateral guarantee facility, particularly by comparison with national schemes.

The concept of guarantees is taken to mean the covering of risks by a special institution in connection with direct investment overseas. As in most countries the granting of guarantees corresponds in purely technical terms to an insurance policy, the terms *guarantee* and *insurance* will be used synonymously throughout.

Guarantee schemes are mechanisms which provide insurance against at least the political risks involved in investment abroad. Whereas *national* systems perform this function only for enterprises of their own (national) economic area investing generally in a closely defined group of host countries, *multilateral* schemes aim to encompass as many investing and host countries as possible; they may be completely open for all eligible countries or restricted to a particular region.

In this study the terms *private investment, foreign investment, direct investment* and *investment abroad* are used synonymously and in a broad sense. They relate to the participation of one or more investing enterprises from one or more home countries in the risk capital of an enterprise in the host country at the time of establishment or expansion with the objective of gaining influence over the business activities of the enterprise. Whether a given minimum capital share is necessary in this context will be examined more closely in the study itself, as will the question whether an insurance scheme should also cover other forms of transfer and participation.

The "Third World" is taken to mean all non-European developing countries. The terms "low" and "middle income countries"
used in the discourse are based on the World Bank definition.

The work is arranged to provide successive analysis of the
situation, the objective and the measures. The first chapter
examines earlier proposals for setting up multilateral guarantee schemes and the reasons for their failure. This is
followed by the development of an economic frame of reference for analysing the World Bank's new proposal; to this
end an attempt is made to determine the essential components
of a multilateral guarantee facility by analysing the aims
of the countries and firms involved. This forms the back-
cloth to the description and analysis of the World Bank proposal set out in the next three chapters. Particular attention is paid to a critique of the premises and to an examination of the elements that can be regarded as essential
components of the new scheme. Besides the actuarial aspects,
the emphasis of the analysis lies mainly on consideration of
the scheme's financial arrangements, its institutional implications and the necessary legal agreements for the protection of investments. On this basis an attempt is then
made to assess the advantages and disadvantages for the
various groups of countries likely to become members - capital-exporting countries with and without national insurance
schemes and capital-importing countries. The conclusion
summarises the main findings of the study and examines the
prospects for the further treatment of the proposal under
discussion and of possible alternatives.

Chapter I: EARLIER PROPOSALS FOR MULTILATERAL INVESTMENT
               INSURANCE AND THE REASONS FOR THEIR FAILURE

§ 1. *Basis of the proposals*

The earlier plans and proposals for the creation of multilateral investment insurance schemes can be traced back primarily to the discrepancy between the ability to export
capital in the form of private investment and the scope for
protecting it against risks, for the most part those of a
political nature. Until 1962 there were only three national
schemes operating in the United States of America, Japan and
the Federal Republic of Germany. Understandably, a multilateral scheme was seen as a possible vehicle of promotion
by all those states that did not have the necessary insurance arrangements.

All the proposals without exception are based on the hypoth-
esis that capital transfers in the form of direct investment
abroad are essential if the international division of labour
is to be intensified and to yield benefits for all those
involved. The need for guarantees is perceived primarily in
connection with investment in developing countries. Over the
years there has been a growing tendency to link development
policy considerations and objectives with the notion of
expanding investment in order to encourage private-sector
co-operation.

The alleged shortcomings of guarantees granted by national
institutions provided another important justification for
the proposals. Apart from the schemes' limited applicability
to a few host countries, the following shortcomings are
mentioned in this connection:

- inadequate coverage of risks;

- failure to provide for newer forms of co-operation that go beyond the traditional direct investment through direct participation in risk capital;

- inability to insure the investments of several investors of different nationalities in a single project (consortium contingency);

- restrictive practices in the granting of guarantees owing in some cases to regional resource ceilings, which affect large projects in particular (geographical coverage).

In addition, national systems were criticised for their administrative cost. Capital exporters also criticised certain technical details of the national insurance schemes, such as the duration of coverage the level of annual premium rates, the administrative procedures for calculating and setting losses and the apparently better facilities available in other systems.

§ 2. *Earlier proposals for multilateral investment insurance*

As early as 1962 a World Bank study on a possible multilateral insurance scheme commissioned by the predecessor to the present-day OECD listed twelve plans.[1] The feature common to them all was that they provided worldwide coverage and were not designed as instruments of regional promotion. This

---

1 See, IBRD, Multilateral Investment Insurance, A Staff Report, Washington D.C. March 1962. The study includes a comparison of the plans drawn up by the Association Internationale d'Etudes pour la Promotion et la Protection des Investissements Privées en Territoires Etrangères (APPI), the Council of Europe, HOOD, JALAN, MAFFRY, OSBORNE, POULZEN, REYRE, STRAUSS, TILNEY-BAGNALL, VAN EEGHEN and ZOLOTAS.

line was further pursued in the World Bank's subsequent proposal to set up an International Investment Insurance Agency (IIIA), which was submitted to the Executive Directors of the Bank for discussion in 1973.[1] The same applies in principle to a paper by the Club de Dakar, which was presented two years ago at the instigation of African academics and politicians.[2] Similar remarks hold good for UNIDO's proposals to set up an industrial insurance system.[3]

The US plan for an International Resources Bank provided for (sectoral) limitation to activities in the commodities field, the main emphasis being laid on the promotion of energy and raw material projects. After discussion in the UN General Assembly (1975), at the Fourth General Conference of UNCTAD in Nairobi (1976) and at the Paris Conference on International Economic Co-operation, the World Bank was asked to study the plan and make proposals for implementation within the framework of the World Bank Group.

Regional proposals for a multilateral scheme have been discussed within the European Communities[4] and the Inter-American Development Bank (IDB). The IDB initiative also envisaged some degree of sectoral limitation to projects in the fields of energy and minerals.

1 See IBRD, International Investment Insurancy Agency, Washington D.C. 16th April 1973.

2 See CLUB DE DAKAR, Proposal by the Club de Dakar for the Establishment of an International Guarantee Fund.

3 See UNIDO, Industry 2000, New Perspectives, Third General Conference of UNIDO, New Delhi, 21 January - 8 February 1980, Vienna September 1979, pp. 236 ff.

4 See EUROPEAN COMMUNITIES, THE COMMISSION, Communication to the Council on the need for Community action to encourage European investment in developing countries and guidelines for such action, (COM(78)23, Brussels 30th January 1978; and Report from the Commission to the Council on investment promotion and protection clauses in agreements between the Community and various categories of developing countries: achievements to date and guidelines for joint action, COM(80)204, Brussels, 8th may 1980.

The Inter-Arab Investment Guarantee Corporation is a regional scheme with a small circle of investing and host countries. It was established in 1966 in accordance with a decision by Arab Ministers of Industry to insure Arab investment in Arab countries against non-commercial risks. This narrow orientation does not accord with the aims upon which multilateral systems are generally founded. Hence the Guarantee Corporation cannot serve as a model for the intended multilateral facility.[1]

All the proposals, including those that operate a fund, are based on the establishment of an insurance scheme to cover risks; actuarial and commercial considerations underlie their design, so that from the technical point of view they present a number of parallels with existing national schemes and a relatively high degree of homogeneity one with another. The differences between these proposals and the national facilities consist mainly in the manner of financing, institutional arrangements and legal safeguards.

The large number of proposals and the discussions about them contrast markedly with the record of implementation. Apart from the Arab scheme, which adopts a different approach, no proposal has yet progressed beyond the drawing board. This is particularly true of the plans of the sixties, but also applies to the global approaches of the IIIA and the International Resources Bank. Work on the IIIA was suspended in 1973 owing to lack of interest among member countries of the World Bank. The difficulties preventing realisation of the proposals also beset the planned granting of guarantees by the International Resources Bank. As a consequence, it was decided to expand World Bank lending in the raw materials and energy sectors rather than set up an insurance facility.

1 This view is also held by the World Bank. See IBRD, Multilateral Investment Insurance Agency, R82-225, 14th July, Washington D.C. 1982, pp. 8 f, paragraph 28 (subsequently referred to as R82-225).

The EC also suspended its activities in this regard, while those of the IDB were reduced to a very low level. In 1980 the IDB did discuss the results of about five year's preparatory work on the creation of an Inter-American guarantee fund to insure foreign investors in the energy and mineral fields against political risks, but the proposals were not approved at the Annual Meeting of that year; instead, it was decided to carry out further studies.

Meanwhile, the number of national systems for granting guarantees has been rising continuously. At present there are twenty-one national investment insurance schemes.[1] All the industrial countries now have facilities of this kind, apart from Ireland and Greece, which are of little significance as exporters of capital, and the European mini-states. Portugal and South Africa are in the process of setting up guarantee facilities. Developing countries such as Korea (1972) and India (1978) have already established national schemes of the own. Hence the only potential capital-exporting countries not covered are the OPEC states with balance of payments surpluses and a few of the newly industrialising countries.

§ 3. *Reasons for non-implementation*

If one looks into the reasons why a multilateral insurance scheme has not yet come into being even though it seems eminently sensible from the point of view of potential capital exporters and might also have advantages for major projects, especially those undertaken by consortia, one finds the same problems time and again. In the eyes of the

---

1 They operate in the following countries: Australia, Austria, Belgium, Canada, Denmark, Finland, France, Federal Republic of Germany, India, Israel, Italy, Japan, Korea, the Netherlands, New Zealand, Norway, Spain, Sweden, Switzerland, the United Kingdom and the USA.

industrial countries as the main capital exporters, they are chiefly as follows:

- The countries have insurance schemes of their own. They may not fully meet the demands made of them in every case, but there is always a degree of interpretive latitude and it is comparatively easy to make applications as the language is the same, personal contacts can be made and so forth. Hence a firm seeking a guarantee sees relatively little need for a multilateral facility. Even if it is a member of a consortium it can insure its own share.

- Measures to promote exports and investment (including the granting of investment guarantees) played an important role in the pursuit of national aims in the foreign trade field after the establishment of a liberal world economic order, for the progressive removal of import restrictions and the prohibition of their reintroduction shifted the scope for influencing foreign trade from import restrictions to the area of export promotion. Investment was seen to be very important in this because of its repercussions on trade. This trend towards incentives for exports of goods and capital was further strengthened by the founding of the EC and the restrictions it placed on member countrie's scope for national economic policies. In the eyes of the industrial countries the transfer of part of their investment promotion activities to a multilateral agency would thus have amounted to forgoing one of their few remaining instruments of influence, which they would have been inclined to do only if the benefit to their own economies could be demonstrated convincingly.

- The legal agreements concerning investment abroad are an important point for both the governments and the firms involved. Under the German scheme, for example, investment promotion treaties made it possible to set high standards that accorded with economic policy objectives and created a yardstick for other countries. In the final analysis such agreements have a decisive impact on the ·long-term settlement of claims and hence on the financial basis and operational viability of the scheme. By comparison with this, the legal agreements were a weak spot in the proposals for multilateral facilities. The reasons for this probably lie in an underestimation of this aspect and partly in the intention of potential multilateral umbrella organisations to demand only relatively modest concessions from host countries (in particular developing countries) in view of possible charges of external interference (or even imperialism). This is particularly true of the calculation of compensation and the reference of cases to internationally recognised arbitration bodies.

- Aversion to a multilateral system also sprang from the judgement that the governing body was bound to lead to excessive bureaucracy because of its special design. Furthermore, some investors felt that there was some danger of the confidentiality of applications being breached if they were no longer processed by a national institution but by representatives of other countries.

For the *host countries* - in particular the developing countries - the proposals for multilateral schemes should have been beneficial, because they should have not only permitted an inflow of capital but also given them access to more modern processes and other know how. However, in practice the proposals met with anything but sustained support. Doubts were concentrated chiefly on the following points:

19

- In the sixties and seventies direct investment and other forms of participation by foreign enterprises were not generally approved by developing countries. Arguments raged about the harmful effects on the economies and policies of host countries. They feared the use of inappropriate technologies, the destruction of indigenous small and medium-sized firms, dominance by foreign firms and hence the infringement of their sovereignty. In many countries this debate was reflected in the introduction of extensive controls and constraints and also led to rejection of the idea of an international court of arbitration. Moreover, many states clearly considered that it was simpler to handle direct investment by means of bilateral agreements with the main capital-exporting countries than to establish arrangements through a multilateral agency.

- During the discussions about the IIIA and the International Resources Bank it became apparent that a large number of developing countries regard the institutionally induced link between traditional multilateral development assistance and private investment as undesirable. In particular, they fear that the creation of a multilateral insurance scheme by the World Bank might affect their general credit standing, as confidential information supplied to the World Bank by individual governments could find its way into the insurance agency's files. Conversely, they suspected that isolated losses on foreign investments could adversely affect the climate for other co-operation projects. Problems were also foreseen in the event that a World Bank organisation lodged claims against a developing country after the occurence of a loss.

- The fact that a multilateral scheme needs to be safeguarded by investment protection agreements did not meet with universal approval. Countries that wish to channel and control investment according to their own national principles feared that a set way of treating foreign private investment would be forced upon them from outside if they joined the multilateral insurance scheme. On the other hand, such agreements did not seem essential to countries that had attracted a large volume of foreign equity capital, for their policy had already been laid down in bilateral agreements and their willingness to perform certain obligations had been duly documented.

A series of further questions remained unclarified from the viewpoints of both *host* and *investing* countries, which sometimes adopted opposing positions. This applies particularly to:

- the additional flow of direct investment to the entire Third World that the introduction of a multilateral guarantee scheme is expected to generate;

- settlement of the question of the political influence of capital exporters and importers through the distribution of votes within the multilateral scheme;

- the entire subject of financing through the inclusion or conscious exemption of host countries.

Overall, there was clearly considerable doubt in the minds of all potential participants about the need, usefulness and long-term effectiveness of a multilateral guarantee facility. Both political and economic considerations played a part in this.

The tabling of a new proposal for such a scheme by the World Bank despite the reserved attitude of many countries in the past and the existence of national investment insurance schemes raises the question whether new prospects have really opened up which show at least some of the previous doubts to be unfounded. To form a judgement on that score one must have a clear understanding of the economic frame of reference. That requires first an analysis of the aims pursued by promoting direct investment through risk insurance measures. On that basis one can then deduce whether a multilateral scheme is required today and what main elements it would have to comprise in order to achieve the desired level of efficiency.

Chapter II: AIMS AND FRAME OF RERENCE OF A MULTILATERAL
               INVESTMENT INSURANCE SCHEME

§ 4. *Aims of the countries and companies involved*

The interest in direct investment stems from the
consideration that world production and income can only be
maximised if the factors of production are used where their
marginal value product is highest. The transfer of financial
resources or entire input packages (which direct investments
are) from countries with low productivity to those with
high productivity contributes to an increase in world production via the reallocation of producer goods this entails.
As the increase in world production ultimately raises pros-
perity in the individual economies, nation states are concerned that cross-border investment should not encounter
difficulties.

The premises on which the theoretical model of worldwide
factor allocation is based do not hold good in practice, so
that direct investment is actually encouraged in most capital-exporting countries. Perfect competition does not obtain
in factor and goods markets, nor do private and social costs
and benefits agree with one another. Moreover, the level of
taxation of profits differs as widely from one country to
another as the standard of the infrastructure. Misallocation
of resources is therefore quite feasible and in individual
countries it may seem that national firms are investing too
little abroad, so that incentives are advantageous. The
expected free enterprise profits can fall far short of the
economically possible returns, particularly where direct
investment in developing countries is concerned. This is due
partly to the considerable political risks to which direct
investors are exposed in developing countries. Guarantee or

insurance schemes for investments in developing countries are therefore among the classical instruments of a promotional policy.

The fact that the premisses underlying the theoretical model are not met often leads capital-importing countries to suspect that too much direct investment might be carried out overall or in specific sectors and industries. If they do not wish to prevent direct investment entirely, these countries then devise a policy to control it and to allow it to have only certain effects. Hence the expectations of capital-exporting and capital-importing countries as to the effects of these movements in inputs are not necessarily the same. The following analysis shows the fields in which their objectives diverge.

The *interests of capital-exporting countries* derive naturally from the over-riding macro-economic aims of full employment, price stability, balance of payments equilibrium and adequate economic growth - the "magic rectangle". However, the lesser objectives pursued in order to achieve these general aims would seem to be more important within the overall aims/means hierarchy, in which direct investment is both a precondition for exports of goods and services and a consequence of such transactions. In many cases foreign investment represents a higher form of merchandise exports and is also an instrument of import and structural policies. The main purpose of encouraging investment in developing countries is to achieve as steady a rise in private investment as possible in order:

- to intensify entrepreneurial activities in existing and/ or new markets so that the potential for additional exports[1] of goods and services from the capital-exporting country can be exploited and markets can thus be diversified, which is also a desirable goal from the point of view of economic activity;[2]

- to secure the supply of vital raw materials;[3]

- to increase the scope for growth in the capital-exporting countries by streamlining industrial structures that have developed along traditional lines or been distorted by subsidies and other support measures.

The latter objective most closely matches the allocation theory considerations, which state that enterprises with below-average productivity in industrial countries should not be kept alive by artificial means. Instead, an appropriate economic policy should be pursued in an attempt to persuade them to transfer production to developing countries, provided factor input and price relations there offer comparative advantages. Being growth industries, they would thus be able

---

1 In this connection see D. KEBSCHULL, Die Wirkungen von Auslandsinvestitionen auf das Beschäftigungsniveau, in: Krise und Reform der Industriegesellschaft, Vol. 2, Frankfurt am Main 1976.

2 The advantages and possibilities of export market diversification from the point of view of the Federal Republic of Germany are described in detail in: SACHVERSTÄNDIGENKOMMISSION "EXPORTFÖRDERUNG BADEN-WÜRTTEMBERG"-EFK, Schlußbericht, Stuttgart 1982.

3 See, D. KEBSCHULL, Nach Energiekrise - Rohstoffkrise? Probleme der Sicherung unerer Rohstoffbasis, Berlin 1981; FRIEDRICH-EBERT-STIFTUNG, Probleme der Rohstoffsicherung - Expertengespräch in Bonn, 26. und 27. Juni 1980, Kurzfassung der wesentlichen Ergebnisse, -- 1980; M. DOMITRA, Krise in der Rohstoffversorgung der westlichen Welt? Expertengespräch in Washington am 11. und 12. Dezember 1980, -- 1981; ITE, INSTITUT ZUR ERFORSCHUNG TECHNOLOGISCHER ENTWICKLUNGSLINIEN, Die Investitionspolitik der NE-Bergbaugesellschaften und ihre Auswirkungen auf die Rohstoffversorgung der Bundesrepublik Deutschland, Hamburg 1978. See also the discussion on the Integrated Programme for Commodities and the so-called Common Fund of UNCTAD; e.g. D. KEBSCHULL, W. KÜNNE, K.W. MENCK, Das Integrierte Rohstoffprogramm, Hamburg 1977; D. KEBSCHULL (ed.), Rohstoff- und Entwicklungspolitik. Wissenschaftliche Schriftenreihe des Bundesministerium für wirtschaftliche Zusammenarbeit, Vol. 28, Stuttgart 1974.

to act as engines of industrialisation in Third World countries and create urgently needed jobs. In the capital-exporting industrial countries, meanwhile, the conditions would be created for a more productive use of labour and capital and hence for faster, growth-inducing structural change. However, there is resistance in the capital-exporting countries to the relative decline in production and employment in the industries affected.[1]

Besides these general economic policy aims, which apply with slight modifications to all Western industrial countries, there are development policy objectives which also work towards increasing the transfer of private capital and in particular direct investment. The broad favour that these aims have again enjoyed in recent years is mainly due to the fact that

- nearly all analyses of the future development of the Third World agree that even a slight long-term narrowing of the gap between "rich" and "poor" will probably require more capital from the industrial countries than was invested during the first two development decades;[2]

- there is only a very slight probability of a lasting increase in official aid (ODA) in the form of resources for

1 See for example H. GIERSCH (ed.), Reshaping the World Economic Order, Symposium 1976, Tübingen 1977; E. HELMSTETTER, Die Chancen der Textil- und Bekleidungsindustrie in hochentwickelten Ländern - Ein empirischer Beitrag zu kontroversen Fragen der Standortsuche beider Industriezweige, Kieler Diskussionsbeiträge, No. 34, Kiel December 1972; G. FELS, Die Textilindustrie und das Theorem der komparativen Kosten - Eine "Erwiderung", Kieler Diskussionsbeiträge, No. 27, Kiel January 1973.

2 Cf. IBRD, World Development Report, Washington D.C. 1982; W. BRANDT et al., North-South, a Programme for Survival: Report of the Independent Commission on International Development Issues, London 1980.

technical and financial co-operation owing to the per-
sistence of worldwide economic difficulties and the
problems in the industrial countries;[1]

- the scope for the developing countries to raise a larger
  volume of capital themselves must be considered to be
  relatively narrow in view of their internal economic and
  structural problems and the rapid growth in private and
  public indebtedness in the last decade.[2]

The *interests of the capital-importing countries* do not
lie so clearly in one direction, although here too the magic
rectangle constitutes the starting point of their reasoning.
After a phase of occasionally excessive criticism of the
activities of foreign enterprises, developing countries are
again opening the doors wider to foreign private investment
in view of the decline in other resources. Apart from the
factors mentioned above, the observation that in recent
years the best growth performances have been achieved by
countries with a high proportion of foreign investment and a
relatively liberal policy towards the transfer of capital
may have played some part in this.

However, what matters to the developing countries is not
simply overcoming bottlenecks in the provision of capital
but also acquiring the other elements linked with investment, such as technical knowledge, management knowhow,
training procedures and advice on opening up and maintaining

1 See C. POLLACK, Neue Formen internationaler Unternehmenszusammenarbeit ohne Kapitalbeteiligung, Munich, Cologne and London 1982, pp. 69
  ff.; OECD, Investing in Developing Countries, Paris, various years.
2 See A. GUTOWSKI, M. HOLTHUS, Limits to International Indebtedness,
  in: D.J. Fair (ed.), International Lending in a Fragile World Economy, The Hague 1983, pp. 237 ff.; M. HOTLHUS, Verschuldung und Verschuldungsfähigkeit von Entwicklungsländern, in: Hamburger Jahrbuch
  für Wirtschafts- und Gesellschaftspolitik, Vol. 26, Tübingen 1981,
  pp. 239 ff.

markets. Nonetheless, they continue to harbour fears of a concentration of foreign capital in the manufacturing field and the possible foreign domination of the economy this could permit.[1] Furthermore the developing countries are often more concerned to expand their own exports and produce import substitutes, aims which in some cases at least are the opposite to what the industrial countries expect from their direct investments. This explains why at the same time as the desire for more private foreign direct investment was being expressed there came fresh demands for greater control over enterprises and entrepreneurs, even to the extent of the demand for nationalisation of foreign property in accordance with national law.[2]

However, justified demands for some degree of control by the host country may be in the light of certain past experience, their overall effect is to impede investment. Potential investors not infrequently equate the voicing of this demand with its implementation and, what is more, assume it applies to all countries. This can so increase the subjective as-

1 This attitude is described in J.-J. SERVAN-SCHREIBER, The American Challenge, London, 1968 with regard to the relationship between the USA and Europe. In the North-South context it is expressed particularly clearly by the representatives of the Dependencia tendency. In this connection see O. SUNKEL, National Development and External Dependence in Latin America, in: Journal of Development Studies, Vol. 6, No. 1, -- 1969/70, pp. 23 ff.; S. AMIN, Underdevelopment and Dependence in Black Africa - Their Historical Origins and Contemporary Forms, in: Social and Economic Studies, Vol. 22, No. 2, -- 1973, pp. 177 ff.; A. SCHMIDT (ed.), Strategien gegen Unterentwicklung - Zwischen Weltmarkt und Eigenständigkeit, Frankfurt and New York 1976.

2 See in this connection the demands for a New International Economic Order in the Charter of Economic Rights and Duties of States, 12th December 1974, adopted by the 29th General Assembly, in: Die neue Weltwirtschaftsordnung, Entwicklungspolitik, Materialien No. 49, Bonn June 1975, pp. 11ff. Cf. D. KEBSCHULL et al., Industrialisierung im Nord-Süd-Dialog - Vorschläge zur dritten Generalkonferenz von UNIDO und Bewertung des Verlaufs, in: Forschungsberichte des Bundesministeriums für wirtschaftliche Zusammenarbeit, Vol. 5, Munich, Cologne and London 1980.

sessment of risk that investment plans are abandoned entirely. Raising the risk threshold would probably prejudice precisely those countries that have either not yet been considered as locations for foreign investment or have attracted only a small volume of investment. Hence these countries and investors from industrial countries have a common interest in measures that will help reduce the risks of investing in developing countries.

Enterprises that have invested in developing countries or intend to set up branches there are primarily concerned to achieve the business aim of safeguarding their earning power over the long term. They expect state incentives to provide:

- as effective a reduction as possible in investment-linked risks;

- risk insurance at low cost;

- clear and administratively simple regulations.[1]

1 Many studies have been made of these objectives, mostly on empirical lines. See inter alia K. SEIBERT, Joint Ventures als strategisches Instrument im internationalen Marketing, Vertriebswirtschaftliche Abhandlungen, No. 23, Berlin 1981; F. GEISEL, Kapitalstrukturen internationaler Unternehmungen, Gießener Schriftenreihe zur Internationalen Unternehmung, Vol. 1, Gießen 1982, p. 24; A. EGLI, Die volkswirtschaftliche Bedeutung des Technologietransfers nach Entwicklungsländern, Birsfelden 1974, pp. 94 ff.; L. HALLEN, International Industrial Purchasing Channels, Interaction and Governance Structures, Uppsala 1982, pp. 33 ff.; H. JÜTTNER, Förderung und Schutz deutscher Direktinvestitionen in Entwicklungsländern unter besonderer Berücksichtigung der Wirksamkeit von Investitionsförderungsverträgen, Internationale Kooperation, Aachener Studien zur internationalen technisch-wirtschaftlichen Zusammenarbeit. Vol. 15, Baden-Baden 1975; K. MORTON, P. TULLOCH, Trade and Developing Countries, London 1977, pp. 231 ff.; F.R. ROOT, Independence and Adaption: Response Strategies of U.S.-based Multinational Corporations to a Restrictive Public Policy World, in: K.P. SAUVANT, F.G. LAVIPOUR (eds.), Controlling Multinational Enterprises. Problems, Strategies, Counterstrategies, Frankfurt am Main 1976, p. 109; S. GERBER, Risikoanalyse und Risikopolitik bei direkten deutschen Auslandsinvestitionen von mittelständischen Unternehmungen in Entwicklungsländern, Frankfurt am Main 1982; OECD, International Investment and Multinational Enterprises. Investment Incentives and Disincentives and the International Investment Process, Paris 1983, pp. 33 f.

Due consideration of the interests of the developing countries plays hardly any role in this catalogue of corporate
aims. In practice, however, the use of insurance schemes
greatly modifies the attitudes of firms owing to the account
taken of the macro-economic aims of industrial and developing countries and the demands stemming from the existence of
market economies in the Western industrialised world.

§ 5. *The main elements of multilateral insurance schemes
from the viewpoint of allocation theory*

a. *Initial considerations*

Whether a national or multilateral insurance scheme meets
the objectives of the capital-exporting and host countries
can be determined conclusively only if a method is developed
that permits schemes with various configurations to be
compared and assessed from the point of view of relative
merit. To that end the links between the aims outlined above
and the steps taken to achieve them must be examined.

Economic policy measures can only ever be assessed by reference to the objectives that caused them to be introduced.
Given the same initial situation, different aims necessarily
require different measures and have correspondingly diver-
gent effects. Development policy objectives place different
demands on a direct investment insurance scheme than the aim
of promoting a country's exports to the rest of the world or
improving the structure of its economy by creating better
conditions for investment abroad. A further factor is that
direct investment itself is already viewed very critically
because of its importance and impact on the aims of both
home countries and host countries. For example, investment
that leads to increased exports by the home country is not

necessarily welcome in a developing country that wishes to substitute imports.[1]

The very fact that the various national guarantee schemes were introduced at widely different times in different world economic situations which also affected each country differently suggests that a variety of aims underlie the national schemes currently in existence. Unless one is prepared to measure each systems against every stated or conceivable aim in turn, a meaningful comparison is not necessarily possible.

Differences in the assessment of the impact of direct investment also make international consensus on the aims and configuration of a multilateral insurance scheme difficult to achieve. They have produced a multitude of proposals but they are probably also responsible for the fact that none has yet been implemented. This failure indicates that not even these considerations can generate a definitive set of criteria from which to deduce the possible superiority of a multilateral guarantee scheme over national arrangements.

Hence practically the only basis for a system of reference by which to compare investment guarantees is the aim of the efficient international allocation of production factors - and in particular capital - that is still generally accepted under GATT and the agreements on the International Monetary Fund. However, it should be remembered that direct investment is not simply a transfer of capital but represents rather a package of capital, technical knowhow and management services.

---

1 See D. KEBSCHULL et al., Wirkungen von Privatinvestitionen in Entwicklungsländern, Baden-Baden 1980, pp. 17 ff.

The requirement to maintain efficient resource allocation
necessarily means that a guarantee scheme should only provide cover against risks that cannot be insured in the market and which therefore impede investment in viable projects. Any insurance cover that goes further than this is in
danger of discriminating against domestic investment, thereby distorting allocation. The allocation objective also
requires adherence to the principle that costs be covered,
as any subsidisation of costs makes the investment projects
in question appear more profitable than they really are. The
consequences would be misallocation of resources and the
wastage of capital.[1]

By considering only the aim of effective factor allocation,
it is possible to reduce the comparison of the various investment guarantee schemes to their main insurance aspects,
such as insurable risks, the amount of claims, waiting periods, etc. All that has to be examined in advance is how
these elements must be arranged in order to ensure effective
allocation. This produces a matrix by which both multilateral and national investment guarantee or insurance schemes
can be assessed.

The use of effective allocation as a yardstick does not mean
that such diverse development policy aims as export promotion on the one hand and import substitution on the other
cannot be achieved. Rather, a country in which investment
projects in the import substitution field are highly profit-

---

1 With regard to incentives in relation to subsidies and the wider concept of protectionism see W. MICHALSKI (ed.), HWWA-Studien zur Exportförderung, Italien (D. KEBSCHULL), Hamburg 1968, pp. 13 ff.; see
  also D. KEBSCHULL, Worldwide Export Promotion Requires New Concepts,
  in: Intereconomics No. 7, 1966, D. KEBSCHULL, Exportförderung als
  Problem nationaler Außenhandelspolitik, in: Gegenwartskunde - Zeitschrift für Gesellschaft, Wirtschaft, Politik und Bildung, Vol. 16,
  No. 1, -- 1967, D. KEBSCHULL, Motive, Maßnahmen und Auswirkungen
  staatlicher Exportförderungspolitik - Das Beispiel Italiens, in:
  Jahrbuch für Sozialwissenschaft, Vol. 20, No. 2, -- 1969, pp. 212 ff.

able will attract direct investment for that purpose. Similarly, a country that offers highly profitable investment opportunities in the export sector will not suffer a lack of foreign capital. The decisive factor, however, is that capital flows should be determined by decisions as to the profitability of projects.

Differences in the assessment of direct investment are the result of adopting a micro-economic view. Of course, only in a very narrow set of circumstances can an individual direct investment simultaneously increase the exports of the home country and reduce the imports of the host country. In macro-economic terms, however, a large number of investments can produce the net import savings expected by the developing country, expecially over the long term. This is most likely to occur if the flow of direct investment is not one-way, but this condition does not yet obtain owing to development disparities. Hence developing countries, in particular, need to channel investment in accordance with their objectives, but the criteria to be applied can only be laid down in each country's authorisation provisions. As we have shown that the aims of the individual developing countries differ widely, an operational multilateral insurance scheme cannot be burdened with this task.

b.   *Essential insurance features*

1.   Eligible investments and industries

At first sight the concept of a direct investment guarantee seems to lay down clearly which external transactions should be given insurance cover. On closer inspection, however, the question arises whether all the transactions carried out in connection with a direct investment actually have to be covered.

According to the IMF definition, the deciding factor in differentiating between direct investment and portfolio investment is whether the investing enterprise can gain influence over the business activities of the recipient enterprise abroad through participation in its risk capital.[1] In the case of plant that have no legal independence, such influence unquestionably exists and it is assumed to be present in the case of capital holdings of 25.1 per cent or more in existing or newly founded incorporated or unincorporated enterprises. However, influence can be established over the conduct of business even with a smaller participation, depending on company law or contractual provisions, so that the holdings must be regarded as direct investment. The provisions governing holdings apply by analogy to the size of flows; capital transferred within a particular period with the intention of influencing the recipient enterprise abroad must also count as direct investment.

At this point the question must be asked whether a guarantee or insurance scheme should grant insurance cover for existing foreign participations and the like or should apply only to new investment. In terms of allocation criteria it can be argued that the risks attaching to existing participations were considered calculable and were incorporated in the profits equation, otherwise the investment would not have been made. In the case of new investment, however, it can be assumed that the investment will not take place if no risks cover is provided. These considerations suggest that a guarantee scheme should offer cover only for new investment.

The re-investment of earnings as risk capital must be regarded as part of the new investment in this connection. Admittedly, it may be supposed that the original investment decision assumed and calculated for a normal expansion, including some accumulation and re-investment of earnings, but the fact cannot be ignored that the nature and composition

34

of risks can change to such an extent over time that re-investment may not take place. Capital increases from the parent company's resources should be treated in a similar way.

Profits obviously do not accrue until the investment has been made and the newly formed or acquired enterprise carried out its planned operations. They are not only re-invested but should ultimately be remitted to the parent company. This too is attended by risks that can cause an investment to fail. Hence a direct investment insurance scheme should also cover the expected transfer of profits from new investments.

These considerations show that a direct investment consists of several stages. On the one hand there is the transfer of the capital contribution to establish, restructure or expand the enterprise and on the other the operational phase with the production and ultimate remittance of any profits. However, it is often overlooked that it also entails a preparatory stage, which can be very intensive and time-consuming, at least in developing countries with ill-defined administrative organs lacking in clear powers. As empirical studies have shown,[1] in some cases several years may elapse between the decision to carry out an investment and the time when all the necessary authorisations have been granted. As a rule, a representative of the firm must be on the spot throughout this period so that the additional information continually required can be provided and further applications submitted. This gives rise to considerable costs, which have a significant impact, especially on small and medium-sized companies. Hence this initial expenditure should be included in the risks cover, if the investor so

1 See D. KEBSCHULL, O.G. MAYER, Deutsche Investitionen in Indonesien, Hamburg 1974, pp. 107 ff.

wishes, thereby possibly mobilising capital from small and medium-sized businesses.

A further problem of definition stems from the fact that direct investment comprises more than the transfer of capital. As a rule it involves transfers of technical and organisational expertise on a considerable scale. If knowhow can be capitalised it is automatically covered with new investment, but such capitalisation is not always possible, so that the payment of royalties to the parent company for these services is attented by risks in the same way as the transfer of earnings. From the allocation point of view it is therefore desirable that management fees and royalties on knowhow deriving from direct investment should be treated in a similar way.

A less clear case can be made out for including loans from the parent to the subsidiary company in developing countries. Such credit relationships frequently exist alongside equity participation to finance the purchase of equipment or as a result of the supply of intermediate products and merchandise by the parent company. This falls outside the classical area of direct investment, for it is no longer a question of whether to include equity capital (which from an economic point of view is risk capital with uncertain yield prospects from the outset) but loan capital at a contractually agreed rate of interest. Where these credit relationships are the result of the supply of goods or services, they can often be secured under export insurance schemes.[1] Hence on methodological grounds financial credits between associated enterprises might not be regarded as eligible for cover under a direct investment insurance scheme.

1 See J. BEYFUSS, Exportversicherung und Exportfinanzierung. Ein internationaler Vergleich, Beiträge zur Wirtschafts- und Sozialpolitik, Institut der deutschen Wirtschaft, 115, Cologne 1983.

Nonetheless, it should be noted in this connection that loans often take the place of equity capital. If that is the case, the payment of interest may indeed by agreed by contract, but it is usually contingent upon a particular outcome, such as the discovery and extraction of mineral deposits, so that the earning prospects can be just as uncertain as in the case of "genuine" risk capital. Moreover, as in the case of direct investment, these loans are often linked with the provision of knowhow and other services. Such non-equity investments are always present if host countries consider that by retaining national control over expected mineral deposits they can obtain higher ground-rents or achieve a better balance of advantages than through taxation or by restricting the level of participation, as in the case of firms in other industries. As the dividing-line between risk capital and loan capital in associated enterprises is therefore fluid, not only non-equity investments but also financial credits between parent and subsidiary companies (provided neither is a bank) should be treated as insurable transactions.

From the points of view of both consistency and resource allocation, pure portfolio investments should be given the same insurance cover as direct investments, for the acquisition of equity holdings of a size that does not permit any influence to be exercised over the enterprise in question should also be regarded as an investment risk capital.[1] However, safeguarding foreign investment against risks is not simply a question of insuring the capital invested; to a large extent it also entails protecting the business activities associated with the transfer of capital. Portfolio in-

---

1 See R.E. GROSSE, Foreign Investment Codes and the Location of Direct Investment, New York 1980, p. 10; R.B. DICKIE, An Examination of Equity Sharing Policies: What Causes Them to Fail - and to Succeed, in: Columbia Journal of World Business, Vol. 16, No. 2, -- 1981, p. 88; K. SEIBERT, op. cit.

vestment does not combine knowhow, management expertise and capital, and for this reason national insurers argue that state insurance schemes should not apply.[1]

Finally, bank loans to foreign enterprises do not fit into this framework, even if their majority shareholder is a domestic company. In this instance the bank will obtain additional guarantees from the domestic parent company. In effect, the credit relationship is therefore between the two associated companies and as such can be covered under the investment insurance scheme. From the bank's point of view such loans do not entail the risks that arise with direct investments. On the other hand, if such loans spring from the financing of goods and services provided by domestic companies to the foreign enterprise, on systematical grounds insurance cover should be available under export credit guarantee arrangements.

2. Policy-holders

A further technical problem derives from the question which natural or legal persons are entitled to take out insurance under a guarantee scheme. The subscribers of equity capital in a direct investment may be one or several enterprises in a foreign country, but they may also come from several countries. It is unimportant whether these include other developing countries. It is also possible, however, that one or several natural or legal persons from the host country itself may contribute to the investment.

---

1 A special OECD committee, the task force on non-concessional flows, recently published proposals that also contemplate insurance cover for pure portfolio investment in developing countries.

The insurance treatment of investors from the host country presents no problems; their share in the risk capital is to be considered a normal domestic investment and not a direct investment. Special insurance cover is not required.

The two other cases are different, however. It must be assumed that the investment will only go ahead if all the parties who consider it necessary can enjoy insurance cover against the investment-hindering risks for which the scheme in question provides protection. Hence, for reasons of efficient resource allocation all investors not resident in the host country must be able to take out policies for their share in the investment.

This line of argument can also be applied to national schemes. If in the case of consortium investments only the investor from one capital-exporting country is granted insurance cover, this merely indicates that the country in question is using its insurance scheme to pursue objectives that go beyond that of effective resource allocation, such as export promotion. Investors from various countries should also be able to obtain insurance cover if they are interlinked, and even if one of the enterprises is a holding company registered in a tax haven. Where national schemes are concerned, all that must be checked is whether the country of residence of the holding company or of another associated enterprise offers the same or similar insurance cover.

3. Eligible host countries

From the point of view of efficient factor allocation it is illogical to exclude particular host countries. The actuarial argument for extending the insurance scheme to as many similar risks as possible so that the probability of loss can be calculated (the law of large numbers) also militates against the exclusion of particular countries. However, if an insurance scheme is regarded as an instrument of development policy, confinement to direct investment and similar capital transactions in developing countries adequately meets that objective.

However, there are other grounds for arguing in favour of the exclusion of certain developing countries. States that present foreigners with an exceptionally hostile investment climate where property is expropriated without compensation indicate by this behaviour that they place no value on direct investment and obviously wish to dissociate themselves from at least this area of the international division of labour. In theoretical allocation terms it is extremely questionable to use an insurance scheme as a means of chanelling risk capital into such countries in spite of this situation. Viewed in this light, it would seem better to provide insurance cover only for investments in countries that meet certain minimum requirements in their behaviour towards a direct investment. Such minimum requirements can be laid down in legally binding agreements for the protection of investments.[1] For example, the arrangements established under the bilateral investment protection or promotion treaties concluded by the Federal Republic of Germany might serve as a model.[2]

4. Insurable risks

Apart from identifying eligible transactions, the central problem of direct investment insurance is defining insurable

1 See H. JÜTTNER, op. cit.
2 In this connection see also sub-section c below.

risks. In the final analysis, the true purpose of a guarantee scheme is to provide insurance against certain risks in order to increase the propensity to invest.

There are basically three separate categories of risks:[1]

(i) *Risks of disasters.* This is interpreted as the danger that the investment may be destroyed or damaged as a result of a natural disaster (volcanic eruption, earthquake, flood, etc.).

(ii) *Political risks.* Here the invested assets, disposition of them or of profits and fees accruing from them are endangered by:

- war, civil war, revolution, insurrection or other armed conflicts in the host country;

- nationalisation or other government action having an effect equivalent to expropriation;

- payment embargoes or moratoria; and

- the inability to convert or remit sums of money.

(iii) *Economic risks.* These comprise:
- the risk of loss as a result of the general economic policy of the country, such as exchange rate changes or other economic measures; and

1 See inter alia S. J. KOBRIN, Political assessment by International Firms, in: Journal of Policy Modeling, Vol. 3, No. 1, -- 1981, pp. 252 ff.; S. GERBER, op. cit.; J.V. MICALLEF, Political Risk Assessment, in: Columbia Journal of World Business, Vol. 16, No. 2, -- 1981, pp. 47 ff.; F.T. HANER, Rating Investments Abroad, in: Business Horizons, -- April 1979, pp. 18 ff.; F.J. JÄGELER, W. WAGNER, W. WILHELM, Radar für Auslandsrisiken, in: Managermagazin, No. 1, Hamburg 1981, pp. 32 ff.; P.J. RUMMEL, D.A. HEENAN, Wie die Multis politische Risiken analysieren, in: Havard Manager, No. III, -- 1980, pp. 46 ff.; W.G. PRAST, H.L. LAX, Political Risk as a Variable in TNC Decision-Making, in: Natural Resources Forum, Vol. 6, No. 2, -- 1982, pp. 183 ff.

- commercial risks, such as miscalculation of the
  sales potential in the host country, bankruptcy of
  local business partners, etc.

A fourth category of risks often also receives specific
mention; these are risks on the borderline between political
and economic risks and for that reason are termed *grey area
risks* in the Federal Republic of Germany. What is meant are
risks that severely restrict control over the enterprise but
do not demonstrably amount to expropriation. Environmental
measures fall within this category, as do regulations on the
proportion of foreign employees in the total workforce or
the level of locally produced intermediate inputs as a proportion of total production, which in some instances are
progressively raised.

In accordance with allocation criteria, which are decisive
from the economic point of view, the risks of natural disaster cannot be insured. Domestic investments are exposed to
the same risks and, moreover, private insurance can be obtained within certain limits.

The eligibility of economic risks can be rejected equally
emphatically. This is especially true of the so-called
commercial risks, but those resulting from general economic
policy also affect domestic and foreign investment alike. In
principle they can be insured in the market, be it with the
aid of third parties (forward transactions, credit insurance, etc.), through self-insurance or by making appropriate
reserve provisions.

The situation is different with regard to political risks,
however. The individual cannot calculate the probability of
the actions and events that trigger them. Moreover, when the
risk occurs, all the direct investments from a particular
economy in the host country are affected, so that the over-

all loss its so large that private insurers are not generally able to provide cover. Hence national or multilateral
insurance schemes with the necessary financial resources
offer to write insurance against these risks.

Grey area risks closely resemble political risks, despite
their economic connotations. If they do occur, they certain-
ly also cause a reduction in the foreign parent company's
control over the subsidiary in the host country. As a rule,
however, action equivalent to expropriation is almost impossible to prove. Hence grey area risks should also be considered ineligible for cover.

It should nevertheless be noted at this point that the need
for certain minimum requirements to be met with respect to
direct investments that was mentioned in connection with the
exclusion of certain host countries also arises with regard
to the definition of types of risks insured. Here too it
makes no sense from the resource allocation viewpoint to
insure against all political risks and thus to evade the
host country's declared policy of hostility towards direct
investment. The proposed exclusion of host countries that do
not meet the declared minimum requirements means that certain political risks and, in particular, grey area risks
will probably not arise.

5. Duration of coverage

The problem of the duration of coverage consists in providing cover against the insured risks for at least long enough
for the invested capital to be amortised. The shorter the
period of insurance, the higher must be the rate of amortisation so that the capital can be amortised within the
period of cover. The shorter the period of insurance, the
greater will be the concentration on the particularly prof-

itable investments in a country. Furthermore, there will be a stronger incentive to avoid taxes in the host country by means of intra-group accounting practices and other measures in order to maintain a high rate of amortisation. Longer periods of insurance may reduce the inclination to resort to such practices and should generally ensure a wider range of investment opportunities. They are therefore in the interest of capital-importing countries.

It is not really possible to lay down an optimum period of insurance for all host countries and sectors. However, previous experience has shown that periods of between 15 and 20 years are generally long enough to ensure amortisation of the capital. As re-invested earnings are to be regarded as new investment, cover will run from a fresh commencement date in each instance. Limiting the period of insurance does, however, disregard the fact that even after amortisation the direct investment represents an asset that may continue to generate profits.[1]

6. Notification requirement and full insurance requirement

Actuarial considerations demand that a notification requirement be incumbent on the policy-holder, in other words that he provides evidence to the insurer that an investment has been made and in what amount. The same applies to proving a loss. The situation is different with regard to the full insurance requirement. Here it is a question whether the policy-holder is obliged to insure all direct investments in countries eligible under the scheme or can himself decide which investments he applies to cover.

1 These problems also arise in valuing losses. See in this connection § 5, sub-section b, 7 below.

An argument in favour of the full insurance requirement is that the insurer thereby obtains a larger portfolio of similar risks and can thus achieve a better mix of risks, which in principle enhances calculability and can reduce the cost of insurance. On the other hand, this deprives the policy-holder of the opportunity to assess the risk himself. Objections to the full insurance requirement can be made on the grounds that the potential policy-holder can no longer choose self-insurance as an alternative to insuring with the guarantee facility. This can lead to a misallocation of resources. Moreover, if full insurance is required, the insurer has no indication of those countries in which direct investments are being made without investors applying for insurance cover. Such a development would show that the risks in these countries had changed to such an extent that they were no longer to be considered eligible for the scheme as the risks could now be insured in the market. A full insurance requirement can probably be dispensed with, as even without it the risks portfolio of a multilateral insurance scheme should be large enough, at least if it is the only institution of its kind.

7.   Insured amount calculation of loss and excess

The *amount of coverage* is important in several respects, for it governs the level of premiums and, in conjunction with the excess, the maximum sum that the policy-holder can expect to receive in the event of a claim. The insured amount is relatively easy to determine at the start of a new investment. The total of the sums invested, the level of expected profits and, depending on the transactions to be covered, the agreed annual premium rate provide the parameters of the insurance policy and hence in the initial stage constitute the basis for determining losses.

As the period of coverage lengthens, however, adjustments must be made in the basis of evaluation of losses. For example, under normal circumstances it can be assumed that at any given time at least part of the investment will have been amortised. This assumption also underlies the limit placed on the period of insurance. In the event of loss the insurer would therefore have to adjust his payments to take account of this development. However, expectations of profits are not always fulfilled; they can be exceeded, but equally often profits do not accrue at all. In the first case the investment is amortised more rapidly and in the second it is not amortised at all. In that case, at any rate, the policy-holder has no interest in basing the loss assessment on a figure lower that the insured amount.

This reasoning disregards the fact that profits are not expected to cease when they have reached the level of the original insured amount. Enterprises rightly work on the assumption that profits should accrue throughout the life of the investment. Hence if the loss is assessed on the basis of amortisation assumptions, in certain circumstances only a fraction of the actual loss may be made good by the insurer.

On the other hand, if the insured amount is always reimbursed in the event of loss, in many cases the insurer will in fact pay not only the loss due to political risks but also that arising from commercial or economic risks. From the allocation point of view this cannot be justified. Furthermore, in an insurance scheme covering only political risks the policy-holder would not have paid premiums for such cover.

Hence the basis for assessing loss should be a "current insured value" which may on the one hand reflect reductions in value caused by business and economic factors but on the other hand also acknowledges the fact that the value of an expropriated enterprise is not nil if it has been increasingly amortised owing to its business success. The current insured value can therefore be higher or lower than the insured amount (which equals the sum invested). If it is higher the loss is calculated from the current insured value, whereas if it is lower the insured amount constitutes the upper limit.

The insured amounts for the individual insurable transactions represent the insurer's maximum liability in the event of loss. However, the question arises whether the policy-holder should not bear some portion of the loss himself. An argument in favour of such an *excess* is that it will make the policy-holder more risk-conscious in his choice of investment projects. Against that, it is very difficult to determine the level of the excess objectively. The argument that an investor will be more carefull in his choice of investment locations if the policy is subject to an excess carries more weight from the viewpoint of efficient resource allocation. In addition, an excess stimulates greater individual effort to avoid or minimise loss. Here too there is validity in the argument that an insurance scheme should not be an instrument to circumvent the economic and growth policy of a country hostile to direct investment. An excess of about 10 per cent seems low enough to be acceptable to the investor and high enough to stimulate risk awareness.

8. Premiums

As stated earlier, any investment insurance scheme should operate on the principle that it covers its costs, as only then will efficient resource allocation be assured. If that condition is respected, the level of premiums is derived from the level of claims in a given period, the probability of loss and the cost of administering the scheme. The method of funding chosen is immaterial in this respect; a combination of the "assessment" and "level premium" methods is probably the best arrangement. The peculiarity of a scheme to insure against political risks is that no loss probabilities can be calculated, so that premiums cannot be set objectively.

Just as important, however, is the question whether premiums should differ according to host country and types of risks insured. The experiences of the private insurance market do favour premium differentiation, but this would entail ranking host countries according to the risks. Such an undertaking is highly charged politically. Hence the most that can be done is to graduate premiums according to insurable risks and transactions. If premiums were to differ according to country they would have to be treated in strict confidence.

9. Occurence of a loss and waiting periods

If a loss occurs, the notification requirement incumbent upon the policy-holder again comes into play; he must inform the insurer and submit evidence of the scale of the loss. He must also show that he has taken adequate steps to avert or minimise the loss.

A period of time (the waiting period) must elapse between occurence of the loss and payment of the claim by the insurer, primarily on the grounds that immediately after the event it is possible in certain cases to have the action reversed or to negotiate compensation from the host country. The length of this waiting period cannot be laid down objectively. It must be long enough to allow the policy-holder to use any scope for negotiation he may have, but it must not be so long that liquidity difficulties and lost interest further increase the total loss incurred. Waiting periods of more than six months appear to serve little purpose. After payment of the claim the right to subsequent reimbursement by the host country should transfer to the insurer. However, whether in the long runs a multilateral insurer can more easily obtain satisfaction of such claims against the developing country is a matter for separate examination.

10. Insurer

The question of the governing body is important, because in an investment insurance scheme providing cover against political risks the level of claims in any given period will presumably not follow the laws of probability. Hence the overall financial requirement cannot be estimated, so that premiums cannot be calculated with sufficient accuracy. No doubt it is for this reason that the risks in question cannot be insured privately. The body responsible for administering a direct investment insurance facility must therefore be an institution with sufficient financial resources to be able to step in if current and accumulated premiums are insufficient to meet claims.

As a rule the only institution that meets this requirement is the state, and it is immaterial whether it assigns administration of the scheme to a private organisation. Should a multilateral scheme be set up, the participating countries would have to assume joint responsibility and make adequate funds available, for the reasons stated.

*Investment protection treaties as an ancillary require-
ment of insurance systems*

An insurance scheme to cover direct investment constructed
in the manner described above will help attract risk capital
into eligible countries if without such a scheme investment
were impeded by the insurable risks. There a string of
countries that are politically so unstable that the ensuing
administrative and economic policy environment deters potential investors. In many of these countries direct investment
would probably be an appropriate instrument to lay the foun-
dation for an efficient structure of production and perform-
ance and would ultimately have a politically stabilising
effect. If an insurance scheme channels investment into such
countries, it is very much to be welcomed on global economic
and developmental grounds.

Not infrequently, however, a tangled web of continually
changing regulations, requirements and authorisation procedures reflects deep-seated scepticism towards foreign investment, or even outright rejection. For whatever political
reason it may be, this attitude is not taken to the ultimate
extreme of prohibiting direct investment. An insurance
facility that also channels risk capital into countries such
as these is highly questionable in global economic terms.
Sooner or later a loss will occur, and the entire project
will prove to be a misinvestment and a waste of capital.

These remarks demonstrate that the international allocation
of goods and resources can only proceed efficiently if the
countries involved so wish and behave accordingly. The party
responsible for causing a loss must be prepared to bear part
of the direct cost of the damage and not only the indirect
costs in the form of lost growth, which is difficult to
quantify. In the direct investment field this means that
potential host countries must demonstrate their good inten-

tions towards such capital flows by meeting certain minimum conditions. At several points in the preceding remarks about the optimum insurance arrangements it has become clear that an agreement on legal rights that is binding in international law is an essential ancillary requirement for investment insurance schemes that are valid on the world scale.

The form that such legal protection takes is immaterial; more important are the minimum requirements it should establish. Experience with direct investment between industrial countries and bilateral investment protection treaties between industrial and developing countries has shown that a small number of basic safeguards are sufficient. Apart from definitional clauses, the agreements must contain legally binding arrangements that ensure:

- That the countries involved do not treat each other's capital investments any less favourably than domestic investments;

- that foreign nationals engaged in capital projects in the countries involved are not treated any worse than domestic citizens as far as their activities are concerned;

- that expropriation is carried out only in the national interest and against due compensation;

- that capital, earnings, the proceeds of disinvestment and compensation can be remitted without delay at the prevailing exchange rate;

- that in the event of dispute the case be referred to an acceptable arbitration body at the request of the investor;

- that account be taken of the principle of most-favoured-nation treatment (or non-discrimination).

The existence of a legal protection agreement does not reduce the insurable risks to such an extent that an investment insurance scheme would no longer be necessary. In addition, it leaves potential host countries enough scope to
channel the capital inflows in accordance with their interests. It does not entirely preclude misallocation of resources, for mismanagement and errors of business judgement
are still possible, but it considerably reduces the danger
that capital will be wasted without regard to losses owing
to the encouragement afforded by an investment insurance
scheme. Hence the principle of efficient factor allocation
can be taken more strongly into account.

In the sections that follow, the World Bank proposal for
multilateral insurance will be described and analysed in the
light of the main insurance features of such a system and
their arrangement from the point of view of resource allocation and subject to the ancillary requirement for adequate
legal protection.

Chapter III: THE WORLD BANK PROPOSAL FOR THE CREATION OF A
             MULTILATERAL INVESTMENT INSURANCE AGENCY

§ 6. *Background and aims*

The plans to establish a multilateral insurance facility,
which have been the subject of many initiatives since the
end of the fifties, gained renewed prominence recently as a
result of proposals tabled by the World Bank. They were presented to the Executive Directors for discussion in August
1982 after consultation with experts in various countries
and with international organisations. Although not all the
details of this new initiative have yet been clarified, the
broad outline of the scheme appears to be relatively settled
within the World Bank. The same holds for substantiation of
the scheme on economic grounds.

In the light of the developments during the seventies described above, the drafting of a new scheme for multilateral
investment insurance and the vigour with which this approach
is again being pursued[1]   come as something of a surprise,
for since the last proposals were made trends have emerged
that seem to militate *against* the establishment of another
multilateral facility.

First, there has been an increase in the number of national
investment insurance institutions and secondly little interest has been shown in such a scheme, even leading the World
Bank itself to abandon work on the IIIA and to shelve other
plans, such as those to set up an International Resources

---

1 See in this connection: A conversation with Mr. Clausen, in: Finance
   and Development, Vol. 19, No. 4, 1982, p. 5 ff.

Bank. In the opinion of the World Bank, both proposals faced a series of difficult questions, particularly in the following areas:

- the link between the World Bank and the institution responsible for multilateral insurance;

- the distribution of voting rights;

- financial participation by developing countries;

- the assignment of claims from the investor to the agency (subrogation);

- arbitration and legal arrangements.

If a new proposal for a multilateral insurance facility is being made despite this far from encouraging experience, the primary reason must lie in developments in the world economy since 1979 and their effects on the developing countries. In its discussion paper[1] the World Bank joins with many other organisations, politicians and academics in assuming that the developing countries have an increased capital requirement.[2] The causes of this are primarily:

- the balance of payments deficits of non-oil developing countries caused by oil and energy prices;

---

1 Cf. R82-225, op. cit.

2 See inter alia IBRD, World Development Report, Washington D.C. 1982, pp. 36 ff. and World Development Report, Washington D.C. 1981, pp. 14 ff.; UNIDO, Industry 2000, New Perspectives, op. cit.; D. KEBSCHULL, Neue Gestaltungsformen und Perspektiven der öffentlichen Entwicklungshilfe, in: SIMONIS, U.E. (ed.), Entwicklungsländer in der Finanzkrise - Probleme und Perspektiven, Schriften des Vereins für Socialpolitik, N.F. Band 136, Berlin 1983, S. 259 ff.

- the high level of interest rates due to US stabilisation policy and the appreciation of the dollar, together with the consequences of this for debt service obligations;[1]

- the rapid decline in commodity prices as a result of the lasting recession in the main consumer countries;

- the danger of a further strengthening of so-called neo-protectionism, which could seriously impair the sales prospects for non-traditional products from developing countries.

The need to mobilise additional capital for the developing countries in this situation is further deduced from the fact that:

- given the existing state of global interdependence, a general recovery in the world economy will only be possible if the developing countries are also included in efforts to generate a worldwide upturn;[2]

- the ODA of Western industrial countries will barely increase in real terms in the foreseeable future;

---

1 On the question of indebtedness see the synoptic treatment in: WIS-SENSCHAFTLICHER BEIRAT BEIM BUNDESMINISTERIUM FÜR WIRTSCHAFTLICHE ZU-SAMMENARBEIT, Stellungnahme zur Auslandsverschuldung der Entwicklungsländer, in: Entwicklungspolitik, BMZ-Aktuell, Bonn April 1983, pp. 7 ff.

2 See, A.W. CLAUSEN, Third World Debt and Global Recovery, The 1983 Jodidi Lecture at the Centre for International Affairs, Harvard University, Boston, Mass., 24 th February 1983 and a summary of opinions in UNCTAD Bulletin No. 192, April 1983, pp. 3 ff.; D. KEBSCHULL, Some Remarks on Proposals for Economic Recovery in Developing Countries, Conference Room Paper No. 7, High Level Expert Group Meetings Preparatory to the Fourth General Conference of UNIDO, Lima, 18th-22nd April 1983.

- private capital transfers and particularly commercial loans are tending to stagnate or decline at present rather than increase in the manner considered necessary.

Against this background, higher priority was again given to the earlier ideas of mobilising a greater volume of foreign capital in the form of direct investment to offset the expected decrease in commercial loans and to secure additional long-term sources of external finance. As the World Bank's report shows, development policy objectives are placed well ahead of global allocation considerations. For that reason the report refers first to the growing difficulties experienced by low and middle-income developing countries in financing their current-account balance-of-payments deficits.

In the view of the World Bank, a concerted effort to create the guarantee mechanism must be made in order to facilitate the flow of private investment to developing countries. The urgent need for comprehensive safeguards against the risks involved (by a multilateral insurance facility) is deduced from the observation that the danger of political uncertainty increases in step with economic instability. The multilateral approach is seen in this context as a prerequisite for ensuring a permanent *additional* flow of resources.[1]

Additionality is expected to produce a gradual and lasting improvement in the investment climate in the majority of potential host countries. It is said that the important point is that non-commercial risks be insured so that firms' decisions are not influenced by factors which from their point of view are practicable incalculable.

Two developments are cited as indicators of the need for multilateral risks insurance. The first is the rapid in-

1 Cf. R82-225, op. cit., p. 1 paragraph 2 (iii) and p. 5, paragraph 12.

crease in the membership of the International Centre for the Settlement of Investment Disputes (ICSID) between 1977 and 1982;[1] the second is the belief that the growing number of national investment insurance schemes in the last decade reflects the growing interest of private-sector enterprises in investment in developing countries. However, as there are "considerable gaps in existing national, regional and private insurance schemes", the multilateral investment insurance company "would be an appropriate facility to supplement these schemes".[2]

The new proposal specifically highlights five points as the most important shortcomings of the national insurance schemes to protect private investment:[3]

- the lack of adequate risks diversification: most countries concentrate investment on a few developing countries with which they have close economic ties. The exposure in individual host countries therefore bears no reasonable relationship to the scheme's reserves;

- increasingly restrictive underwriting policy: this is partly the result of the above-mentioned regional concentration of private investment on a few developing countries. The attempt to avoid such regional imbalance had meant, among other things, that large-scale energy and mining projects in particular could no longer obtain sufficient cover;

- difficulties in writing insurance for investments of mixed nationality: this seems to be particularly significant in the case of energy and mining projects, as the

---

1 Ibid., p. 5. paragraph 11 (at the time of the report ICSID had 81 Contracting Parties).

2 See R82-225, op. cit., p. 1, paragraph 2 (iv).

3 Ibid., pp. 7 f., paragraphs 21-27.

large capital sums required for such investments are having to be raised to an increasing extent by international consortia. "Parallel insurance" of each investor by his respective national scheme is possible, but would lead to unacceptably high administrative expense owing to the duplication of negotiations on contracts and any losses, particularly if different laws had to be applied;

- difficulties with re-insurance on the private market; here it is argued that owing to their poor risks distribution the portfolio of national schemes can be re-insured with the private market only at high cost and on unfavourable terms, if at all. Use of this facility would spread their risks and alleviate their strucural problems (i.e. regional imbalance), but re-insurance would only be available at prohibitive cost as long as the structural problems remained;

- the lack of national investment insurance agencies in certain capital-exporting countries: this deficiency affects primarily the surplus OPEC countries, whose investors have an urgent need for insurance according to the World Bank.

Shortcomings in regional and private facilities are also cited to further bolster the case for establishing a multilateral scheme. The only regional system in operation - the Inter-Arab Investment Guarantee Corporation - is criticised on the grounds that since its insurance is limited to the Arab states it cannot contribute towards the promotion of private investment in developing countries in general.

It is conceded that the private insurance market greatly increased its turnover and underwriting potential between

1973 and 1982,[1] but there still remained typical bottlenecks that private insurers were hardly in a position to
alleviate. The report mentions the lack of cover for war
risks, limitation of cover to three years[2] and the high
premiums in comparison with those of national schemes.

Against this background, the advantages of a multilateral
insurance agency are considered to lie mainly in the following areas:

- the insurance of investment from countries that have no
  national facility of their own;

- the provision of cover for investment from countries
  whose national schemes are overexposed, for example
  because of a regional bias;

- co-insurance of major projects with national schemes;

- re-insurance and co-insurance with the private market,
  permitting a wider risks diversification than in the case
  of national schemes, the avoidance of restrictive underwriting practices, the encouragement of potential investors and hence the mobilisation of additional capital;

1 Premiums from insurance against political risks amounted to about $ 2
  to 3 million in 1973, with the maximum size of an insurable project
  being about $ 8 million. According to the World Bank, in 1982 premium
  income totalled $ 40 million and it was possible to insure single
  projects of $ 200 million or more. See R82-225, op. cit., p. 9,
  paragraph 29.

2 There is the possibility of renewal, but the report states that this
  offers the investor less security than the fifteen-year coverage
  provided by most national schemes. See ibid., p. 9, paragraph 30
  (ii).

- inclusion of consortia through the insurance of investments in which enterprises from several countries are involved.

The possibility of bringing about a lasting mobilisation of additional capital by means of the proposed new facility is regarded in an entirely positive light. The report does stress that the scale of the additional investment cannot be predicted, as the assessment of political risk is but one of many factors influencing investment decisions abroad, but it states that such risks might constitute a barrier to otherwise commercially sound investments. Adequate risks cover would gradually improve the investment climate in the developing countries. In order to facilitate a lasting additional flow of resources all "non-financial and non-commercial"[1] risks have to be removed. One means to that end would be the multilateral investment insurance scheme.

§ 7. *Main elements of the proposal*

The plan for the "Multilateral Investment Insurance Agency" (MIIA) has only been discussed in outline within the World Bank so far, so that there is a series of technical details that must still be regarded as relatively open. This makes it difficult to describe the proposal precisely, but on the other hand a fairly clear picture of the intended facility can be gleaned from the arguments put forward to justify the new scheme, the criticisms levelled at the existing facilities and the information on preliminary consultations.

The range of *insurable investments and sectors* clearly covers all foreign direct investment. It is unclear how far other non-equity investment is to be included. However,

1 See R82-225, op. cit., p. 13, paragraph 46.

60

judging from the economic grounds advanced to justify the proposal, the main emphasis will probably be placed on the transfer of capital. No restrictions are proposed - with regard to eligible sectors.

Enterprises in any country can be *policy-holders*. The proposal lays particular stress on the inclusion of enterprises from developing countries, in particular capital-exporting countries among the newly industrialised and OPEC states. The participation of eastern bloc countries is not expressly ruled out. However, given the nature of the proposed governing body, the provision of insurance is tied to membership of the World Bank.

The circle of *eligible host countries* is narrower than that of some national systems, for only investments in developing countries are to be covered. The primary aims are to avoid the restrictive effects of country ceilings and a regional accummulation of risks by holding a wider portfolio and to realise development advantages for a larger number of host countries.

The *insurable risks* would usually be those of a political nature only.[1] Three categories are mentioned specifically:

- expropriation, confiscation or equivalent governmental action or inaction which deprives the insured investor of effective control over or the benefits of his investment;

- politically motivated restrictions on the conversion or transfer of the host country's currency;

  - armed conflict and civil unrest.

1 See R82-225, op. cit., p. 13, paragraph 46.

In addition, it might be possible to insure other non-commercial risks "having serious adverse effects on international investment".[1] This aspect is not explained further. Insurance would be provided only if all countries involved agreed.

No set *duration of insurance* is suggested. However, from the general context it is clear that the agency would follow the practice of the national schemes.[2] Hence coverage should last fifteen years, or possibly longer in individual cases.

There is no *requirement* for firms *to insure all their investments* in developing countries. As the multilateral facility is intended to complement existing arrangements, investors from countries with a national state or privately-run scheme should therefore always have the choice between this and multilateral insurance. The *requirement to provide information* on the characteristics of the transaction to be insured seems all in all to correspond to the requirement to notify national insurance institutions. However, co-operation between these institutions and the body responsible for the multilateral scheme gives rise to peculiarities.

In order to simplify administrative procedures, the powers of the multilateral agency would be delegated as far as possible to the existing national institutions, which would screen applications in accordance with the agency's guidelines and general business conditions. If necessary and desired, the multilateral agency can provide technical advisers in order to ensure uniform processing and treatment

1 R82-225, op. cit., p. 13, paragraph 46.
2 This can be inferred from the remarks about the shortness of private insurance cover and the comparison with national schemes. See ibid., p. 9, paragraph 30 (ii) and p. 6., paragraph 17.

of applications. As well as this arrangement, under the present proposal the agency would retain the right to undertake its independent assessment of the risk factors and of the impact of investments on its own portfolio.[1] Consequently, the advantage of providing information to only one institution, which is emphasised particularly in regard to small and medium-sized firms, would probably be whittled away by additional reporting requirements.

No restrictions are mentioned with respect to the level of the *insured amount*. The proposal is clearly designed both to mobilise greater investment by small and medium-sized enterprises and to remove the present financial impediments to large-scale investments in energy and mining by actively promoting these sectors. For large projects the scope for co-insurance with a national insurance scheme or private insurers and syndicated insurance would be exploited.

Arrangements with regard to *earnings* are not specified. It must be assumed that technical arrangements will be found that correspond to those applied by national schemes for the various types of insurable investment. There is little danger of discrimination against national systems.

The scale of *annual premiumrates* is also one of the matters that are still open. Differentiation according to host country - in line with the assessment of risk - does not seem to be proposed; indeed, this would ill accord with the role of the World Bank as a potential governing body, which must maintain a high degree of neutrality in the judgement of political developments and must respect countries' sovereignty in this field. Nevertheless, it would be conceivable to graduate premiumrates according to the level of economic development of the host country. This would match the grad-

1 See R82-225, op. cit., p. 15, paragraphs 55 f.

uation of lending conditions, which is already practised, but in some cases it would probably conflict with the actuarial principles of national schemes.

In any case, a multilateral scheme would also aim to keep premiumrates as low as possible in order to make the facility attractive and to mobilise a sustained flow of additional capital. A large portfolio across a broad sectoral or regional spectrum should ensure the necessary risks diversification and re-insurance with private underwriters should as far as possible avoid the need to draw on limited sources. The same objective is served by the reduction in the administrative cost of a worldwide scheme by means of the proposed co-operation with national institutions. Premium income and the special arrangements on the settlement of claims are intended to ensure that the multilateral agency would be financially self-supporting after an initial period.

As in the case of premiums, *ascertainment of the case of a loss* and possible *waiting periods* are among the technical matters which would probably be set by analogy with national arrangements once interested parties had agreed on the principles of the scheme. The proposals regarding the *settlement of claims* are unusual, however, for the idea of "sponsorship" entails a joint liability on the part of investing countries to meet losses that has not been applied up to now.

The underlying idea of "sponsorship" is that losses would be borne by all investing countries in the scheme in proportion to their share in the insurance issued - very similar to the principle of "pay as you use". For example, if investment cover of $ 100 million, $ 50 million and $ 50 million have been granted to the three countries A, B and C respectively, country A has a 50 per cent share in the scheme and countries B and C shares of 25 per cent each. In the event of a

64

loss they are liable in these proportions. Hence, if a $ 10 million loss is incurred, A would bear $ 5 million and B and C each $ 2,5 million.[1] Their liability would be reduced if the agency had re-insured the risk. There is no provision for host countries to bear a proportion of losses.

As the degree of risk attaching to individual investments differs, the possibility is also raised that national insurance institutions sponsoring particularly risky investments would have to bear a larger proportion of any loss on those investments than their percentage share of the portfolio would indicate. As an alternative, it is being considered whether the national scheme should insure a "significant part" of the investment on its own account.[2] This would be tantamount to an excess at a higher level.

According to the present proposal the *institution responsible for the scheme* would be the World Bank. What is envisaged is a legally independent agency with its own juridical personality but which would operate under the auspices of the Bank and with its support. The link between the insurance agency and the Bank could consist in:[3]

- the use of the World Bank's specialist expertise and administrative support on an ad hoc basis;

- enhancement of the reputation and standing of the new organisation through membership of the World Bank Group;

- conclusion of a management agreement to take permanent advantage of the Bank's expertise;

1 See R82-225, op. cit., p. 13 f., paragraph 48.
2 Ibid., p. 15, paragraph 57.
3 See R82-225, op. cit., pp. 14 f., paragraphs 51 ff.

- systematic use of the results of the Bank's dialogue with borrowing countries;

- the use of World Bank personnel, at least initially.

As the agency's financial requirements would be met by premiumrates and "sponsorship", the organisation itself would have no major financial problems. Members of the scheme would incur no liability until they sponsored investments for insurance under the scheme. Only in the initial period might it be necessary to levy a contribution on all member countries to cover administrative expenses until the system was self-supporting.[1] The funds required might even be provided by the Bank within the framework of the "link" between itself and the insurance agency.

As mentioned above with reference to the notification requirement, the umbrella organisation would co-operate closely with the existing national insurance bodies on the institutional level. As it is customary in international organisations, the agency would have a supervisory board on which developing and industrial countries (or host and capital- exporting countries) were represented. The representation of both groups of countries is regarded as an essential prerequisite for improving the climate between capital-exporting and capital-importing countries. If there were a large number of members, each country would not have its own representative; this corresponds to the arrangements that prevail in other development organisations.

Responsibility for day-to-day operations would be vested in an executive management, with fundamental decisions remaining the preserve of a higher supervisory board. The voting structure would be such that countries with the greatest

1 Ibid., p. 13, paragraph 47.

obligations towards the agency had the most voting rights. Such an arrangement is considered essential to attract the support of capital-exporting countries. At the same time non-capital-exporting countries would have to be assured of "appropriate representation"[1] in order to safeguard the interests of all parties.

The principle that voting rights would be determined largely by the scale of involvement might not be applied during the initial period in order to avoid imbalance in the distribution of voting power. Here too, the capital-importing developing countries would be assured a minimum number of votes, although the proposal does not define this more precisely.

The question of *legal protection* is one of the most difficult aspects of this multilateral scheme. In view of the fact that all national schemes provide for measures to ensure that they do not ultimately take over the liabilities of host countries at the expense of their own taxpayers,[2] the World Bank proposal also stresses the need for arrangements of this kind. It emphasises on the one hand that the principle of sponsorship should not entail rolling over the risks and obligations from host countries to the group of capital-exporting countries. On the other hand, in pursuing its claims the agency would have to maintain strict respect for the sovereignty of host countries and, moreover, must not reduce international standards of investment protection.

The possibilities are considered:

- The host country would have to expressly approve the insured investment, accept the general insurance conditions

1 See R82-225, op. cit., pp. 16 f., paragraphs 61 f.
2 Ibid., p. 17, paragraphs 63 ff.

and undertake to compensate the agency. The legal relations between host country and agency could be laid down in an umbrella agreement, which could also provide for the referral of disputes to international arbitration.

- Alternatively, investors themselves could be required to conclude an investment contract embodying the rules of the International Centre for the Settlement of Investment Disputes (ICSID). In the event of a loss they would then have to exhaust the possibilities of ICSID before turning to the multilateral insurance agency.

The extent to which the second alternative might also be coupled with an "umbrella agreement" is not discussed.

Although a number of the more technical details have yet to be settled, the *main features* of the multilateral insurance facility may be *summarised* as follows:

- the multilateral facility complements the existing insurance and guarantee schemes;

- all capital-exporting and capital-importing countries are free to join;

- until insurance is issued, the member incurs no obligations - apart from the possible need for an initial contribution - to cover the cost of administration during the start up period;

- policy-holders' obligations towards the system arise in the shape of premium payments and as a result of the principle of sponsorship;

- the scheme's governing body maintains a close link with the World Bank and makes use of the existing institutions in individual capital-exporting countries in order to exploit available expertise and reduce administrative costs;

- co-insurance with national schemes is envisaged in order to avoid restrictive effects that may be present;

- both co-insurance and re-insurance will be sought with the private insurance market in order to reduce the multilateral facility's capital requirement in the event of losses;

- capital-exporting and capital-importing countries are represented in the organisation. Voting rights are allocated in proportion to investing countries' liabilities towards the scheme. A guaranteed minimum number of votes is reserved for host countries;

- legal protection for investment is considered essential. A binding arrangement is not yet being proposed.

Chapter IV: ASSESSMENT OF THE ESSENTIAL PREMISSES

At first sight, the scheme outlined by the World Bank has appealing features. It conveys the impression that with its aid the aspirations of capital-exporting countries, enterprises and capital-importing alike can be met. Not only does it appear to be beneficial to existing national insurance schemes but it also opens the way for integrating private insurers into a comprehensive worldwide scheme for guaranteeing investments in developing countries. The facts that members incur no obligations and that administrative costs will be kept to a minimum as a result of the link with the World Bank seem particularly attractive *prima facie*.

Given this wealth of advantages, it seems remarkable that not one of the many similar multilateral guarantee schemes proposed in the past has yet been implemented and that both investing and host countries have reacted cautiously. The proposed system will therefore be examined more closely in the chapters that follow. The appraisal is based on the assessment matrix outlined above. The following additional points will also be examined:

- the requirements and assumptions that had a decisive influence on the design;

- the shape of selected components of the system and their economic and development policy implications;

- the scheme's possible impact on capital-exporting countries with and without national insurance schemes and on the capital-importing developing countries.

Only in the light of this assessment can judgement be passed on the suitability of the multilateral facility to produce a lasting increase in foreign private investment in developing countries and to provide effective safeguards.

The assumptions that probably carried most weight in the drafting of the World Bank proposal relate to:

- the need to reduce the developing countries' current account deficits by providing a permanent additional source of funds;

- apparent clear shortcomings in the structure of national investment insurance schemes and their limited field of application.

§ 8. *Reduction in the balance of payments deficits of developing countries*

The World Bank's finding that the balance of payments problems of developing countries have become much more acute since the second rise in oil prices as a result of the continuing world recession and the measures individual industrial countries have taken to overcome it finds general acceptance. However, the global portrayal of the situation for low and middle-income countries as economic justification of the porposal glosses over the diversity within these groups of countries as well as the fact that this development was also partly due to widely differing domestic factors in each country.

To the extent that the causes of the present crisis are of a temporary nature they can be counteracted adequately by

using the IMF instruments[1] and by adjusting domestic economic policy.[2] Furthermore, where there are structural
longer-term disequilibria, a change in the direction of
national economic policy appears to be essential.

As the economic difficulties of many countries of the Third
World necessarily lead to a general deterioration in their
income position, there is probably justification for the
expected stagnation or even decline in commercial lending to
these countries, particularly if at the same time they lack
an economic policy aimed at stability and growth.

It is more than doubtful, whether in such circumstances
insurance against political risks can be expected to produce
the permanent increase in foreign private investment the
World Bank would like to see. Studies into the motives for
such investment agree that they are made primarily with a
view to the medium and long-term earnings potential.[3]
Sales-oriented investment, which predominates in the
majority of capital-exporting countries[4]

1 See D. KEBSCHULL, Alternativen internationaler Entwicklungsfinanzierung, in: H.-B. SCHÄFER (ed.), Gefährdete Weltfinanzen, Bonn 1980,
  pp. 47 ff.

2 On the need for domestic adjustment in developing countries in the
  current situation see WISSENSCHAFTLICHER BEIRAT BEIM BUNDESMINISTE-
  RIUM FÜR WIRTSCHAFTLICHE ZUSAMMENARBEIT, Stellungnahme zu den Vorschlägen des Zweiten Brandt-Berichts, in: Entwicklungspolitik,
  BMZ-Aktuell, April 1983.

3 With regard to motivational research, see in particular J.H. DUNNING,
  The Determinants of International Production, in: Oxford Economic
  Papers, New Series, Vol. 25, New Jersey 1973, pp. 295 ff.; A. AL-ANI,
  Deutsche Direktinvestitionen in Entwicklungsländern, in: Wirtschafts-
  dienst, Vol. 49, No. 4, Hamburg 1969; R. JUNGNICKEL, G. KOOPMANN,
  K. MATTHIES, R. SUTTER, M. HOLTHUS (eds.), Die deutschen multina-
  tionalen Unternehmen, Frankfurt am Main 1974.

4 The USA is to some extent an exception in this respect; see H. KRÄGE-
  NAU, Internationale Direktinvestitionen, Ergänzungsband 1978/79,
  Hamburg 1979 and Ergänzungsband 1982, Hamburg 1982.

and as a rule consists in investment by manufacturing industry in the consumer and capital goods fields, is therefore
directed chiefly towards countries with a high purchasing
power[1] and favourable growth prospects. The expectation of
relatively low political risks is an implicit requirement
for the investment. If a multilateral facility reduces the
political risks in countries that do not offer adequate
earnings potential, the effect on the most important para-
meter of the investing enterprise's decision, namely the
expectation of profit, is very slight. Hence a lasting
increase in investment in previously neglected host countries is hardly likely to occur.

By contrast, supply-oriented investment in the raw materials
fields - in particular in the mining and energy sector - is
relatively independent of the economic situation in host
countries. In view of the long lead time of such investment,
political risks are probably a significant factor in the
decision. On the other hand, it should be borne in mind that
the developing countries have built up a large number of
guidance and control mechanisms, particularly in the extractive sector, so that a lowering of the threshold of political risk is unlikely to lead to a substantial increase in
investment in this sector. In addition, investments of this
kind are highly dependent upon the infrastructure possessed
by the country concerned. Hence a reduction in political
risks is a sensible and necessary measure, but it can hardly
be deemed sufficient to mobilise additional capital.

The same is true of the aim of directing a larger volume of
investment capital towards the group of low and middle-income developing countries with balance-of-payments deficits.
Up to now, these countries have been of secondary importance
as investment locations, mainly because of their weak pur-

1 See D. KEBSCHULL et al., Wirkungen von Privatinvestitionen in Entwicklungsländern, op. cit.

chasing power and low level of development, which also leads
to bottlenecks in many areas of significance for production.
The results of investigations in this field all show that
directing foreign investment into particular countries by
means of government incentive measures has met with little
or no success so far.[1] This general finding with regard to
individual measures.[2] Hence the claim that the scheme
proposed by the world Bank:

- could reduce the balance-of-payments-deficits of developing countries by increasing the inflow of investment capital, and

- was designed to achieve a broader regional diversification of direct investment, particularly by exploiting the
  possibilities of investment in the poorer countries,

appears to be exaggerated, at the very least.

If it is assumed that capital is invested where the yield is
highest, the reduction of political risks would be a suitable means of mobilising foreign resources for a large number of investment projects of above-average profitability.
In reality, however, there would seem to be grounds for se-

1 See H.E. SCHARRER (ed.), op. cit.; D. KEBSCHULL et al., Wirkungen
   von Privatinvestitionen in Entwicklungsländern, op. cit., p. 158; H.
   JÜTTNER, op. cit. This was also acknowledged by the Federal German
   Government in 1981, when it terminated government incentives for
   German investment in developing countries by passing the second
   Budget Structure Law; see Steuerliche Entwicklungshilfe läuft aus,
   in: Nachrichten für Außenhandel, 15. 9. 1981.

2 The small impact of fiscal incentives is clear from the German Development Aid Law and the Developing Countries' Taxation Law. In this
   connection see K.W. MENCK, Möglichkeiten steuerlicher Förderung von
   Investitionen in Entwicklungsländern, in: Staatsfinanzierung im
   Wandel. Verhandlungen auf der Jahrestagung des Vereins für Socialpolitik, Gesellschaft für Wirtschafts- und Sozialwissenschaften in
   Köln 1982, Berlin 1983, S. 619 ff.

riously doubting whether abundant investment opportunities exist. Moreover, it cannot be overlooked that political risks constitute only *one* of several obstacles to investment in developing countries. Administrative barriers and other restrictions are of least equal importance in these countries.[1] A large-scale mobilisation of capital requires the removal of all these impediments and hence in many cases a fundamental revision of economic and social policy. However, these are precisely the fields in which the World Bank will probably show little inclination to exert influence.

All things considered, therefore, the objective of reducing balance of-payments-deficits represents a rather unsuitable starting point for justifying a multilateral investment insurance scheme on economic and development policy grounds. The same goes for the one-sided emphasis laid on the transfer of capital, for the developmental value of foreign involvement does not lie solely or even primarily in the import of capital by the host country but in the associated transfer of technical and managerial expertise, knowledge about the organisation of production, marketing possibilities and training effects. It is these that make state encouragement of foreign investment in the countries of the Third World seem justified on development grounds. However, this aspect is not considered in the World Bank proposal. To this extent, it lays itself open to the criticism that it is merely an additional instrument for the massive transfer of resources sought by the developing countries.

---

1 See inter alia A.-J. HALBACH, R. OSTERKAMP, J. RIEDEL, Die Investitionspolitik der Entwicklungsländer und deren Auswirkungen auf das Investitionsverhalten deutscher Unternehmen, Munich and London 1982, pp. 59 ff. and 156 ff., and D. KEBSCHULL, O.G. MAYER, op. cit., pp. 105 ff.

§ 9. *Shortcomings of the national investment insurance schemes*

The World Bank's criticism of the national schemes causes one to ask whether:

- the configuration of these special incentive measures in general or individually (still) meets the requirements of private-sector co-operation in a world economy oriented towards a greater division of labour;

- any discernible disadvantages call for corrective measures

- such corrective measures are possible within the framework of national policies to encourage foreign investment, and whether

- they make the establishment of a multilateral guarantee facility appear more meaningful from the points of view of economic and development policies.

a. *Analysis of the individual elements*

1. Eligible investments and industries

All of the existing insurance schemes were originally designed for the classical capital investment in an enterprise. As subsidiaries wholly owned by parent companies are increasingly the exception rather than the rule owing to the measures taken by developing countries,[1] they now apply

---

1 With regard to the problems of joint enterprises and the reduction of risks see inter alia F.R. ROOT, op. cit., p. 108; M.G. GILMAN, The Financing of Foreign Direct Investment: A Case Study of the Determinants of Capital Flow in Multinational Enterprises, London 1981, p. 15; J.R. de la TORRE, Export of Manufactured Goods from Developing Countries: Marketing Factors and the Role of Foreign Enterprise, in: Journal of International Business Studies, Vol. 2, No. 1, 1971, p. 31; R.B. DICKIE, op. cit., pp. 88 ff.

generally to:

- participations in foreign enterprises;

- non-equity loans made in addition to equity participation;

- the provision of capital for branches and factories.

In most systems remitted *earnings* can also be included. Japan permits credits to be insured, provided they are linked to a direct investment.

With the growing importance of other non-equity forms of investment the insurance instruments are being adapted to meet the needs encountered in practice. This applies first and foremost for *licensing agreemnts* and service contracts. The schemes run by all countries except France, Belgium and Switzerland expressly provide for insuring licences and royalties, at least if they can be treated as assets.[1] However, even in these three countries the existing regulations could be interpreted as permitting the insurance of this form of collaboration.

Since 1977 it has been possible to insure so-called *service contracts* in the Federal Republic of Germany. This facility has been used only in the field of petroleum extraction so far, where the traditional concession or participation is being replaced increasingly by service contracts, with the producer country retaining full rights of ownership and exploitation over potential production. Under the forms of this type of co-operation practised so far the partner from the industrial country finances exploration and development of the deposit. In return, the oil-producing country agrees:

1 If they cannot be treated as assets, they may be eligible for export insurance, for example in Canada.

78

- to allow him to take a share of production for a specified period on preferential terms and also to reimburse his expenses by means of deliveries of oil (service contract); or

- to sell him a share of production on specified terms without reimbursing past expenses (production sharing).

The Canadian scheme allows contracts for technical services in general to be insured.

The need for insurance in connection with co-operation projects in developing countries also goes beyond the forms outlined above if the industrial country grants the recipient enterprise *untied financial loans.* If such loans are extended by the participating enterprise and provided the lender is a non-bank, they can be insured under the German scheme because they are assumed to be quasi-equity investments. Untied financial loans granted by banks are only covered if they are made to the bank's subsidiary companies.[1]

In recent years there has been much discussion of whether insurance should not also be available for the various forms of *technology transfer,* as they are to be regarded partly as a substitute for a true equity investment. However, this problem appears less significant from the point of view of the economies concerned, as they effect almost all of their technolgy transfer in close conjunction with exports or direct investment,[2] for which insurance can already be obtained.

---

1 Untied financial loans by banks to other enterprises in developing countries are not insured under the German investment guarantee scheme; other appropriate instruments are available for this. In other countries the distinction cannot be clearly discerned.

2 See K.W. MENCK in collaboration with R.E. SCHWARZ, Technologietransfer in Entwicklungsländer - Der Beitrag deutscher Unternehmen, Hamburg 1981.

Hence it can be seen that some existing national schemes insure new forms of co-operation against increased risks as well as wholly-owned foreign branches and joint ventures, so that the complaint that they are not in a position to take adequate account of new types of relationship appears to be utterly unfounded. The criticism can be sustained only to the extent that there is naturally some delay for administrative reasons before the schemes can be adapted and expanded in response to actual developments. More important, however, appear to be differences in assessment of the need for expansion. This became clear in the example of service contracts in the Federal Republic of Germany, where the traditional mining sector, as opposed to the oil industry, has evidently seen no need up to now to conclude and insure such contracts. It is probable that investors elsewhere also see no need to secure new forms of participation such as these on account of the industrial structure in their countries.

As far as the various successive phases of an investment are concerned, it will be found that expenditure on *planning and preparation* is not included in the insured amount, except in the capital-intensive exploration for mineral oil deposits. Administrative and economic considerations endorse such an exclusion only in the case of costs incurred before finalisation of a particular project.

A comparison across the various national investment insurance schemes does not reveal discrimination against individual sectors. Only the interest of banks in a reduction in risks appears to be neglected as a result of the exclusion of their untied financial loans. As stated above, this appears justified on systematic grounds, as such loans are not risk capital and they can generally be insured in another way, as in Germany. At most, only the extension of insurance to other forms of co-operations calls for discussion. Apart from this, the types of insurable investment and the inclusion of all relevant sectors give little cause for criticism of the national schemes or proposals for improvements. This picture might change, however, when the range of eligible policy-holders has been examined.

2. Policy-holders

The schemes in existence today are unquestionably designed to safeguard the interests of investors from their own economies. Without exception, they insure only enterprises of their own country against the risks of investing abroad. They do not yet make provision for possible investment by firms of various nationalities. This can give rise to serious problems if the high capital requirements in sectors such as mining and oil exploration induce enterprises from several investing countries to form a consortium but one member cannot obtain insurance. Differences in the insurance facilities available to investors under different national schemes can also prove a hindrance. In view of the possible increase in the importance of raw materials projects, consideration should be given to widening national schemes to include the coverage of multinational consortia.

From the actuarial point of view such insurance appears quite feasible, particularly as a national scheme can avoid overexposure by re-insuring or making other arrangements to spread the risks. On the other hand, considerable difficulties arise in the event of a loss, for then the various insurers would have to negotiate individually with the country responsible. Not only would this entail great administrative cost, but the damage paid would differ widely in accordance with the various investment protection agreements. Hence it

is doubtful whether a solution that is even half-way satisfactory can be achieved in this manner.

The insurance of investment made via a holding company registered in a third country appears to be equally problematic. That such cases are not unimportant is shown by the
fact that according to data published by the Deutsche Bundesbank one-quarter of German foreign investment in 1979 was
channelled via holding companies and investment companies
domiciled abroad.[1]

The arguments against covering such investments in a national investment insurance and guarantee scheme include the
following:

- holding companies are usually established outside national territory in order to realise particular business
  advantages; hence no reason can be seen why they should
  also benefit from the advantages of the legislation and
  economic policy of their (former) mother country;

- investments are often made in low-tax countries for pur-
  poses that are not basically in tune with the economic
  objectives of the insuring country.

If, on the other hand, one begins from the assumption that
the fear of political risks, expropriation, transfer difficulties, etc. is the main obstacle to a worldwide increase
in investment, in particular for projects in developing
countries, a different line of argument can be followed.[2]

---

1 See DEUTSCHE BUNDESBANK, Die Kapitalverflechtung der Unternehmen mit
  dem Ausland, in: Monatsberichte der Deutschen Bundesbank, Vol. 33,
  No. 1o, 1981, p. 43; G. KAYSER, B.H. KITTERER, W. NAUJOKS, U.
  SCHWARTING, K.V. ULLRICH, Investieren im Ausland. Was deutsche
  Unternehmen draußen erwartet, Bonn (no date), pp. 11 f.

2 See A Conservation with Mr. Clausen, op. cit., pp. 5 ff.

For if that is the case, there are cogent reasons why even holding companies might modify the regional and sectoral distribution of their investments to the benefit of previously neglected countries if facilities to reduce the risks were available.

From the purely technical point of view it would be quite feasible to have holding company investments insured by national schemes. In the event of a loss, however, the holding company, its country of residence and the insurer would have difficulty asserting their claims. The questions of legal protection and subrogation are so unclear in this context that the provision of cover by national agencies does not seem possible at present.

In all the national schemes the provision of cover does not depend on the *size* of the policy-holding enterprise or that of the firm involved in the host country. Any deliberate encouragement given to investments by small and medium-sized enterprises on general economic and development policy grounds is provided through special measures.[1]

As the question of safeguards for foreign investment is treated predominantly from the perspective of the capital-exporting countries and often still on the basis of hundred-per cent equity holdings, the reduction of risks is of very minor interest to the foreign partner in a joint venture, who is becoming increasingly important as this form of business spreads from the extractive sector to other industries. The industrial countries' promotion schemes take no account of his interest in protection. A background consideration

---

1 For this purpose the Federal Republic of Germany not only provides market and country information but also makes loans to encourage German firms to establish branches in developing countries and provides facilities through the Deutsche Finanzierungsgesellschaft für Beteiligungen in Entwicklungsländern (DEG).

was presumably that the partner can insure his share with the insurance agency in his own country. However, where partners are from other developing countries this can fall down owing to the lack of effective institutions or the relatively high premiums because of the low level of development of the insurance sector. Furthermore, it is far from certain that the additional risks perceived as particularly onerous by a foreigner will actually be covered by insurance institutions in Third World countries. This applies in particular to the group of political risks that also constitute a barrier for investors from the developing country itself. Hence insurance schemes tailored for enterprises in capital-exporting countries take only limited account of the aim of generally reducing the risks attendant upon investment in developing countries.

3. Countries coverage

Whereas Australia, Austria, Belgium, Japan, Norway and the United Kingdom insure capital investments in industrial and developing countries, the schemes operating in Canada, Denmark, the Netherlands and Switzerland relate only to investments in developing countries as laid down in the guidelines applied by the United Nations and accepted by the OECD.

Certain restrictions on country eligibility operate in France, Sweden, the Federal Republic of Germany and the United States of America. In France the BFCE usually writes insurance only for projects in developing countries with which France has investment protection treaties and which belong to the franc area as well as for mining projects in OECD countries. Investments in other countries are assessed from case to case. COFACE guarantees, by contrast, are not restricted to particular regions.

Swedish investment insurance is limited to capital invest-ments in countries that are recipients of bilateral official aid. Since 1980 these countries have comprised primarily Tanzania, Vietnam, India, Mozambique, Zambia, Bangladesh, Sri Lanka, Kenya, Zimbabwe, Angola, Ethiopia, Botswana, Guinea-Bissau, the Lao People's Democratic Republic, Cape Verde, Pakistan, Lesotho, Somalia and Swaziland.[1]

The German scheme requires basically that risks be insured only in the case of investments in developing countries with which there are investment promotion treaties or which offer some other form of legal protection, such as through their legal system.[2] At present 42 agreements of this kind have come into force and a further eight treaties have only been signed (see Tables 1 and 2).

Investment promotion treaties between industrial and devel-oping countries of the kind concluded by Germany are of great importance, because in this way host countries them-selves to a mode of good conduct and thus greatly influence the investment climate for foreign activities in their coun-try. By concluding agreements of this kind the host country expresses its willingness to protect foreign investments.

As a rule the treaties lay down that:

- capital investments from the country of the contracting party shall no be treated any worse than domestic invest-ment of investments from third countries (non-discrimina-tion);

1 See Schweden, Entwicklungshilfe von 1 % des BIP vorgesehen, in: Nach-richten für Außenhandel No. 21 of 30.1.1981; Schweden bleibt bei hoher Entwicklungshilfe, in: Frankfurter Allgemeine Zeitung No. 9 of 12.1.1982.

2 This applies mainly in the case of insured investment in Latin Ameri-ca.

Table 1: The Federal Republic of Germany's investment promotion treaties in force of 1st January 1983

Countries	Date of signature	Publication of ratification law in Bundesgesetzblatt	Date of entry into force
Cameroon	29.06.1962	1963 II. p. 991	21.11.1963
Central African Rep.	23.08.1965	1967 II. p. 1657	21.01.1968
Chad	11.04.1967	1968 II. p. 221	23.11.1968
Congo (People's Rep.)	13.09.1965	1967 II. p. 1733	14.10.1967
Ecuador	28.06.1965	1966 II. p. 825	30.11.1966
Egypt	05.07.1974	1977 II. p. 1145	22.07.1978
Gabon	16.05.1969	1970 II. p. 657	29.03.1971
Greece	27.03.1961	1963 II. p. 216	15.07.1963
Guinea	19.04.1962	1964 II. p. 145	13.03.1965
Haiti	14.08.1973	1975 II. p. 101	01.12.1975
India (intergovernmental agreement)	15.10.1964	Bundesanz.No.235 of 16.12.1964	15.10.1964
Indonesia	08.11.1968	1970 II. p. 492	19.04.1971
Iran	11.11.1965	1967 II. p. 2549	06.04.1968
Ivory Coast	27.10.1966	1968 II. p. 61	10.06.1968
Jordan	15.07.1974	1975 II. p. 1254	10.10.1977
Korea	04.02.1964	1966 II. p. 841	15.01.1967
Liberia	12.12.1961	1967 II. p. 1537	22.10.1967
Madagascar	21.09.1962	1965 II. p. 369	21.03.1966
Malaysia	22.12.1960	1962 II. p. 1064	06.07.1963
Mali	28.07.1977	1979 II. p. 77	16.05.1980
Malta	17.09.1974	1975 II. p. 1237	14.12.1975
Mauritius	25.05.1971	1973 II. p. 615	27.08.1973
Morocco	31.08.1961	1967 II. p. 1641	21.01.1968
Niger	29.10.1964	1965 II. p. 1402	10.01.1966
Pakistan	25.11.1959	1961 II. p. 793	28.04.1962
Portugal	16.09.1980	1981 II. p. 56	23.04.1982
Rwanda	18.05.1967	1968 II. p. 1260	28.02.1969
Rumania	12.10.1979	1980 II. p. 1157	10.01.1981
Saudi Arabia (agreement on the protection of rights)	02.02.1979		15.03.1980
Senegal	24.01.1964	1965 II. p. 1391	16.01.1966
Sierra Leone	08.04.1965	1966 II. p. 861	10.12.1966
Singapore	03.10.1973	1975 II. p. 49	01.10.1975
Sri Lanka	08.11.1963	1966 II. p. 909	07.12.1966
Sudan	07.02.1963	1966 II. p. 889	24.11.1967
Syria	02.08.1977	1979 II. p. 422	20.04.1980
Tanzania	30.01.1965	1966 II. p. 873	12.07.1968
Thailand	12.12.1961	1964 II. p. 687	10.04.1965
Togo	16.05.1961	1964 II. p. 154	21.12.1964
Tunisia	20.12.1963	1965 II. p. 1377	06.02.1966
Turkey	20.06.1962	1965 II. p. 1193	16.12.1965
Uganda	29.11.1966	1968 II. p. 449	19.08.1968
Yemen	20.06.1974	1975 II. p. 1246	19.12.1978
Zambia	10.12.1966	1968 II. p. 35	25.08.1972
Zaire	18.03.1969	1970 II. p. 509	22.07.1971

Table 2: Investment promotion treaties of the Federal Republic of Germany that have been signed but had not entered into force by 1st January 1983

Country	Date of signature	Publication of ratification law in Bundesgesetzblatt	Applicable on a provisional basis
Bangladesh	6.5.1981		yes
Benin	(usw.)		no
Israel		1978 II p. 209	yes
Lesotho			no
Mauritania			no
Oman			no
Papua-New Guinea		1982 II p. 389	yes
Somalia			no
		total: 8 treaties	

Note: Treaties were also originally signed with Chile, Columbia, Ethiopia, Ghana, Kenya and the Philippines, but there is no longer any prospect that they will come into effect.

- the capital investments enjoy protection and security;

- if at all, nationalisation or expropriation will be carried out only in return for adequate compensation and that the legality of the expropriatory measure and the level of compensation can be reviewed by an ordinary court of law;

- capital, profits, interest, loans, the proceeds of liquidation and compensation can be remitted without hindrance;

- disputes that cannot be settled between the contracting parties shall be referred to binding arbitration.

By ensuring that foreigners are treated in the same way as nationals and providing for most-favoured-nation treatment, compensation and the free remittance of capital, the promotion treaties constitute an essential precondition for the risks to be at least approximately calculable and hence insurable. The USA has also concluded agreements with 114 developing countries, although they do not match up to the standard of the German investment promotion treaties. Almost all US investments in developing countries are thus eligible for insurance cover.

Overall, it can be concluded that the industrial countries' existing guarantee and insurance schemes do not discriminate among developing countries, at least as far as investment areas are concerned. The conclusion of additional investment promotion treaties by the United States and Germany shows that the industrial countries are making a sustained effort to create better conditions for direct investment in Third World countries but do not wish knowingly to accept the danger of capital wastage.

On the other hand, non-discrimination against certain countries reflects the lack of special and deliberate promotion of countries or country groups by means of the guarantee instrument. To the extent that they make provision for it in their development policy, the industrial countries attempt to achieve this objective by means of other incentives and through the general stance of development policy.[1]

---

1 In the case of the Federal Republic of Germany particular mention may be made here of the former Developing Countries Taxation Law or the terms for loans to encourage German firms to establish branches in developing countries; another aspect is the often repeated attempt to concentrate technical co-operation in the poorest developing countries. See BUNDESMINISTERIUM FÜR WIRTSCHAFTLICHE ZUSAMMENARBEIT; Deutsche Unternehmen in Entwicklungsländern - ein Handbuch für Lieferungen, Leistungen, Investitionen, 2nd edition, Bonn May 1982.

4. Types of risks insured

The national systems give a relatively diverse picture with regard to the actual purpose of insurance arrangements, namely the coverage of certain risks in order to increase the propensity to invest. Of the three categories of risk pertinent in foreign trade (risks of natural disasters, political and transfer risks) they generally cover only events caused by political intervention. According to the German definition, which is echoed in other countries, this cover extends to:

"(a) nationalisation, expropriation, intervention tantamount to expropriation or unlawful failure to act on the part of the government or other authorities having an effect equivalent to expropriation (expropriation contingency.);

(b) war or other armed conflict, revolution or insurrection (war contingency);

(c) payment embargoes or moratoria (moratorium contingency);

(d) impossibility of converting or transferring amounts deposited with a solvent bank for transfer to the Federal Republic of Germany (CT contingency)".[1]

Only Belgium provides cover against natural disasters. Other schemes take the realistic view that such risks could be borne by other (private) insurers. The possibility of insuring against economic and, in particular, commercial risks in

---

1 See clause 4 of the Allgemeine Bedingungen für die Übernahme von Garantien für Kapitalanlagen im Ausland (July 1978 version), published by Treuarbeit AG.

the form of the insolvency of the foreign partner exists only in Switzerland under the state insurance scheme. However,
the guarantee applies only if the debtor is a "public
authority".

Most schemes insure the domestic investor by granting cover
against all named risks. In the USA, however, each risk can
be covered separately. This naturally has an impact on the
incidence of loss and on the level of premiums. Such differences in potential cover can obviously prove a constraint
where several foreign investors of different nationalities
are involved in the same project. If the present practice is
retained, this obstacle can be reduced only if joint supra-
national harmonisation or co-ordination bodies are created
and endowed with adequate powers. There would also have to
be complete clarity about the handling of individual arrangements, as they might deviate considerably from the
formal provisions.

Problems arise with insurance against measures tantamount to
expropriation resulting from the general economic policy of
developing countries - in particular special regulations on
private investment - and which seriously restrict the foreign shareholder's influence and control over the affairs of
the business. Advocates of cover for these so-called *grey
area risks* consider the need for such measures to be particularly acute in the case of investments in developing
countries. They felt that their case was strengthened in the
late sixties and early seventies, when they believed they
had detected a growing aversion amoung the representatives
of many developing countries towards investment by multinational enterprises. They saw the proposals for establishment
of a New International Economic Order as further confirma-
tion of the urgency of their demands, particularly the emphasis on national sovereignty and the right to absolute
control over the country's own resources, in conjunction

90

with the proposal to be able to expropriate foreign companies according to national law and without involving the International Court of Justice.

Although this argumentation is realistic in some respects, particularly in the context of that period, the question arises whether such intervention should be the subject of guarantees of insurance cover. The following considerations inter alia, argue against this line:

- the imposition of special regulations on foreign firms is a permanent feature of policy towards foreign investment in many countries. If this is set out in ordinances or laws and is known to the entrepreneur before the investment is made, it cannot be the place of state promotion mechanisms to intervene here;

- entrepreneurs often exaggerate with regard to state intervention, as it generally restricts their scope for decision-making. This is true, for example, of regulations to reduce the staff of foreign technicians and managers, to lay down capacity ceilings or impose environmental conditions.

In cases such as these one can scarcely speak of a true grey area risk. This occurs more when an investor receives official assurances that are subsequently broken in a discriminatory way owing to political developments.

In principle, this situation comes very close to the definition of political risks. It therefore appears to be acceptable that investors can now insure such risks under the German guarantee scheme. It should be emphasised, however, that the quasi-expropriatory action must always be connected with the breaking of official assurances. Other forms of grey area risk simply involving changes in general economic policy do not come under this heading.

The negative attitude towards foreign capital and other influences did not intensify further in the second half of the seventies. As a growing number of developing countries were, in fact, competing for additional private foreign investment, this subject has declined in importance.

5. Duration of coverage

As with all individual measures, the provisions with regard to the period for invoking guarantees also differ quite widely from one country to another. The guarantee period lasts:

- a maximum of 20 years in Austria and Norway;

- 15 years at most in Australia, Belgium, Canada, Denmark, France, Japan, the Netherlands, Switzerland and the United Kingdom; and

- at least five years in Norway.

Variable periods are laid down only in the USA, Sweden and the Federal Republic of Germany:

- the investment guarantee in the United States runs for a maximum of 20 years for small investments that are considered certain and no more than 12 years in the case of large and sensitive projects;

- in Sweden and the Federal Republic of Germany the normal maximum period is 15 years. However, in individual cases it can be extended to 20 years (e.g. for oil projects in Germany).

From the technical point of view and in terms of consistency, the periods of cover can be considered satisfactory on the whole, despite differences between the national schemes. The maximum periods of cover should generally be long enough to ensure amortisation of the capital invested and the profits retained in the early years. Explicit differentiation according to size of project and degree of risks as in the US scheme seems unnecessary when viewed from this angle, as the potential maximum duration can easily be shortened to suit the case in hand.

The long insurance periods do not raise problems from the viewpoint of the developing countries either. Unless internal country differentiation provides otherwise, they prevent discrimination among potential host countries and a concentration on "early capitalistic" investments with an extremely short capital recovery period. Such a concentration could not be avoided if there were no insurance or if it were of short duration.

The fact that arrangements are satisfactory from the actuarial and development points of view is an essential condition, but it is not necessarily a sufficient prerequisite for greater private investment in most developing countries. This depends first and foremost on investment opportunities, and in particular on the prospects for profits.

6. Notification requirement and full insurance requirement

None of the existing systems require private investment abroad in particular foreign countries to be insured against particular risks. The main reasons are probably that:

- even without compulsory insurance the portfolio of risks should be large enough to ensure calculability and to permit a reduction in the risk;

- investments in industrial countries require no insurance cover if overseas investment is to be guaranteed primarily against politically inspired risks.

Quite apart from the fact that compulsory insurance does not seem justified on economic grounds, its value for developing countries as investment locations is also difficult to see. They would probably be far more concerned that their image as a host country should not be impaired by an insurance requirement imposed by a guarantee agency.

As befits the individual treatment of applications, the insurers decide whether to grant a guarantee on the merits of the case. This is justified from the point of view of the insurer, as political and economic developments in individual developing countries make underwriting seem pointless during certain periods. This practice could, nevertheless, be criticised by developing countries; however, such criticism would be justified only if insurers discriminated deliberately and blatantly against certain countries in their examination of insurance applications. A charge of discrimination cannot be sustained if certain countries openly violate the principles of legal protection for foreign investment or clearly indicate their intention of doing so.

In that case they must accept the consequences of the lack
of guarantees and the absence of investment.

7. Coverage in case of loss

The insurance payment that the policy-holder can actually
expect in the event of a claim depends on the insured
amount, the value on which calculation of the loss is based
and the share of the calculated loss that the policy-holder
must himself bear. The differences between the national
schemes lie mainly in the valuation approach for assessing
losses and the excess.

In the Federal Republic of Germany, for example, the coverage of the loss is based on a so-called "current insured
value" in Deutsche Mark obtained from the material value at
the time of the loss plus or minus the value of capitalised
income. As a rule, the policy-holder himself bears five per
cent of the total or partial loss calculated on this basis,
although in many cases, such as oil projects, he may bear up
to 30 per cent. Indemnity cannot exceed the value of the
original capital investment (the insured amount), but at the
request of the policy-holder the insured amount - and hence
the maximum indemnity - can be increased at no extra cost by
up to 100 per cent of its original value by capitalising retained earnings. The compensation paid under a claim can
therefore quite easily amount to 200 per cent of the original capital investment.

In the United Kingdom, the United States, Australia, Denmark, Japan and Austria the loss is calculated by analysing
balance-sheet values. In Belgium, Canada, France, the Netherlands, Norway, Sweden and Switzerland the balance-sheet
values or the insured amount are reduced in process of time
on the assumption that amortisation has taken place. This

is either determined case by case (e.g. in Canada, Belgium or the USA in the case of large projects) or on the basis of an agreed scale of amortisation (France, Norway and Switzerland). Years free of premium are generally granted (3 to 10 years).

As in the Federal Republic of Germany, most other schemes permit investors to incorporate re-invested earnings in the cover. This is done, for example, in Australia, the United Kingdom, Canada, New Zealand and the USA on the basis of annual stand-by declarations. The coverage of retained earnings therefore varies according to expected profits and retention policies. Here too the upper limit for the inclusion of retained earnings is usually 100 per cent of the original capital investment.

The policy-holder's excess on losses calculated in this way is set at the following levels in the remaining countries:

Country	per cent	
Australia:	10-25	(reviewed every three years)
Austria:	0,10-30	for high country risks
Belgium:	10	
Canada:	15-20	
Finland:	10	at least
France:		
COFACE:	5	
BFCE:	10	
India:	10	sometimes more
Israel:	10	
Italy:	30	
Japan:	10	in the case of financial loans 20 per cent
Korea:	10	at least
Netherlands:	10	
New Zealand:	10	
Norway:	10	
Spain:	10-20	
Sweden:	10-20	
Switzerland:	30	
United Kingdom:	10	
USA:	10	

Service contracts are usually subject to a higher excess; in Germany this is 30 per cent. The excess is higher still for *loans* linked to investments. Here Japan and other countries operate on the basis of 50 per cent.

Upper limits are also set for distributed *profits*. These differ widely; for example, in Germany cover is provided for eight per cent per annum, subject to an overall maximum of 24 per cent of the insured amount. Similar provisions apply in Denmark and Sweden. In Japan 10 per cent per annum is eligible for a period not to exceed the lifetime of the investment value. By contrast, the upper limits for coverage of retained profits stand at 200 per cent in the USA and the United Kingdom and 150 per cent in Canada.

The reasons for the differences described above lie both in insurance considerations and in economic policy arguments. Most of the institutions responsible for insuring risks are required to cover their costs. The US insurance scheme must even show long-term profits on its commercial activities.[1] For these reasons at least, the insurance bodies have an interest in encouraging policy-holders to choose their investments carefully and to help minimise any loss by having them bear part of it. In addition, by writing down the value of the investment (the insured amount) they ensure that the system's ability to function is not impaired by early exhaustion of the ceiling that is often set (Table 3 lists the ceilings for various countries).

---

1 See THE OVERSEAS PRIVATE INVESTMENT CORPORATION, A Critical Analysis Prepared for the Committee on Foreign Affairs by the Foreign Affairs Division, Congressional Research Service, Library of the Congress, 4th September, Washington D.C. 1973, pp. 11 ff.

Further constraints on behaviour that pays too little regard to risk are built into all national schemes. These consist in:

Table 3: Maximum guarantee commitments in various industrial countries in 1977 (in millions of US-dollars)

Country	Ceiling
Australia	245
Belgium	23.5
Canada	250
Denmark	330
Japan	1,350
Norway	750*
Sweden	100
Switzerland	220
United Kingdom	650
USA	7,500

* This amount applies to investment and export guarantees.

Source: OECD, Investing in Developing Countries, Fourth Revised Edition, Paris 1978, pp.12 and 13.

- premiums for the granting of a guarantee;

- the periods that must elapse between occurrence of an insured loss and final payment of the claim, which may lead to serious liquidity problems, depending on their length.

In addition, firms generally have alternative investment opportunities in other countries and other forms. Risk assessment therefore always plays an important role in decision-making.

Claims by the advocates of developing countries' interests that these states are primarily interested in more private co-operation and that this is constrained by arrangements such as the excess and the partial transfer of risks onto the investor do not stand up to examination. By pursuing appropriate policies these countries can ensure that direct investments are exposed to as little political risk as possible.

Viewed as a whole, it can be seen that policy-holders in various countries must reckon with very different treatment in the event of a claim. Discrepancies are not large between the important capital-exporting countries of Germany, the United Kingdom, Japan and the USA, but in the other countries investors might wish for better indemnity. However, this more advantageous promotion of investment must not necessarily be part of a multilateral scheme.

8. Level of premiums

The cost of insurance can be deduced from the annual premiums, the excess in the event of a claim and, indirectly, the method used to calculate the amount of indemnity. The level of premiums also differs from one national scheme to another, in some cases considerably.

Most industrial countries charge flat-rate premiums; these are 0.5 per cent in Denmark, the Federal Republic of Germany, Norway and Austria, 0.55 per cent in Japan, 0.7 per cent in Sweden, 0.8 per cent in the Netherlands and 1 per cent in Canada and the United Kingdom. On top of this there are non-recurring handling charges (as in Germany) or supplements for the inclusion of certain transactions and risks. For example, in the United Kingdom a commitment premium of 0.5 per cent per annum is charged on the stand-by amount and Japan levies an additional 1 per cent premium to cover credit risks.

Australia, Switzerland and the USA apply differentiated rates of premium. The Australian procedure gives joint ventures beneficial treatment by reducing the normal premium from 1 per cent per annum to 0,8 per cent per annum if the local partner holds at least 25 per cent of the enterprise's capital. In addition, Australian investors must pay between o.3 and 0.4 per cent on half the stand-by amount. In Switzerland premiums differ according to whether capital contributions or the remittance of earnings are to be insured. As a rule participations attract a premium of 1.25 per cent per annum and earnings 4 per cent per annum calculated on the volume of expected profits.

In the USA basic premiums differ according to the industry and supplements or rebates are then calculated on the basis of the particular risk profile. Basic premiums are 0.30 per cent for restrictions on remittances, 0.60 per cent for expropriation and 0.60 per cent for war risks. The premium for the stand-by amount is set at 0.25 per cent per annum.

It is clear from even this brief summary and the remarks on the valuation of losses and the policy-holder's excess that there are considerable differences in the cost of insurance cover for firms from different industrial countries. As the investments generally involve relatively large sums, insurance costs are a weighty factor in spite of the apparently low rates. This might indicate that policy-holders in certain countries would have a strong interest in greater standardisation of insurance terms. However, it should be noted that the different rates of premium also reflect differences in the costs incurred by the guarantee institutions, so that standardisation of premiums is not acceptable from the point of view of efficient resource allocation. All that can be standardised are the principles governing the level of premiums, such as the manner of differentiation, etc.

From the development viewpoint, standardisation on the Australian scheme's differentiation favouring participation by local partners should be the ovjective.

None of the schemes expressly provide for premium differentiation according to host country, although this does not rule out the possibility that supplements are applied in practice to certain groups of countries. These could be abolished if the countries in question adopted the investment protection agreements mentioned above.

9.   Occurence of a loss and waiting periods

One of the greatest problem areas in all schemes to insure risks on overseas investment is the treatment of claims. The various schemes appear to describe the occurence of the insured event clearly, but losses are assessed individually in the same way that applications are examined case by case. The claimant must be able to prove that he has done everything in his power to avert or reduce the loss; in other words, where appropriate he must have attempted to obtain adequate compensation. How difficult this is in practice can be judged from the fact that foreign enterprises in a developing country are not all expropriated simultaneously but at intervals. Obtaining this proof alone normally takes a considerable time.

For this reason most guarantee schemes provide for a waiting
period between occurence of the loss and the payment of indemnity. In the German system, for example, this is two
months for conversion or transfer risks. It is precisely
this "CT contingency" that demonstrates the purpose of the
waiting period. It would hardly be efficient to set in
motion the process of examination and possibly payment by
the insurer in cases where settlement by the developing
country is possible and probable within a short time. On the
other hand, the insured firm would suffer considerable expense as a result of lost cash-flow if it had to wait for
the procedure to be fully completed before receiving payment
from the insurer. The waiting period is designed to do justice to both points of view.

As a general rule all rights to subsequent compensation from
the host country pass from the policy-holder to the insurer
upon payment of the indemnity. It is assumed that it will be
easier for an official guarantee institution to assert its
remaining claims against a developing country than for an
individual company. Hence the waiting period and the assignment of rights are to be viewed in conjunction with ohne
another.

The whole set of problems relating to the processing of
claims could be greatly simplified for enterprises and
guarantee institutions if:

- developing countries recognised their obligation to pay
  compensation for expropriation and other politically-mo-
  tivated interventions;

- if capital-exporting and capital-importing countries
  jointly recognised a supreme arbitration body within the
  framework of multilateral investment protection agreements where appropriate bilateral agreements had not been

concluded. A multilateral investment guarantee alone brings no advantage.

The *governing bodies* of the national investment insurance schemes under review are either state institutions or state-controlled agencies. In Australia, Canada, France, Norway, Sweden, Switzerland and the United Kingdom they are closely linked with export credit guarantee institutions. Only in Denmark has a new body been set up in connection with official development assistance.

The advantage of such an institutional arrangement is primarily that sudden large losses need not threaten the existence of the scheme, as the state can step in with guarantees, loans and so forth without granting subsidies. For the same reasons, the insurance institution need not react by immediately raising premiums; this becomes necessary only if difficulties persist over a long period. Hence a stable business policy can be pursued.

A certain disadvantage with this arrangement may be seen in the fact that the interests of the insuring countries take priority over those of the developing countries. However, this need not be the case by any means, as explained at several points above.

b. *Overall assessment of the national schemes*

The growth in the membership of the ICSID and the fact that an increasing number of national systems have come into existence are cited as evidence of the need many countries and enterprises feel for a multilateral facility. However, neither reason can be regarded as convincing grounds for establishing such a scheme. As there was no lack of proposals and plans for multilateral guarantee institutions during the period in which the national schemes were developing, the growth in the number of national schemes tends to indicate their superiority. At any rate, it would seem that from the point of view of the countries concerned it was easier to set up a scheme of this kind than to join a multilateral agency.

The interpretation of the development of national investment insurance schemes gives the impression that the issue is being argued with a steady eye on a particulate aim and not at all objectively. This is also true of the catalogue of alleged shortcomings of the national schemes which, naturally, are not perceived in a multilateral facility and, it is claimed, can be completely rectified by creating such an agency.

As mentioned above in describing the main technical aspects of insurance, the crucial determinants in assessing the promotional instrument under discussion are the overriding objectives, which are regarded as absolute. If efficient resource allocation is acknowledged to be dominant objective, a critique calling national systems in general into question does not appear justified, for the basic principles to be observed in operating such a promotion scheme can as a rule be considered to have been satisfied, both from the point of view of those wishing to invest abroad and on actuarial grounds.

It therefore seems perfectly feasible to modify and complement the various elements in such a way that the schemes pay still better regard to the allocation objective and the more commercial insurance requirements. As regards the developing countries' demand for more capital to be mobilised through private investment - including quasi-equity participations -the existing national schemes merely constitute a necessary but far from sufficient condition. Fulfilment of this demand requires not only the above-mentioned changes in insurance details but also and above all fundamental measures by the countries themselves to improve and stabilise the investment climate. The fact that this entails commitments was underlined in the examination of bilateral investment promotion treaties and in the repeated references to a multilateral investment protection agreement.

There can be no doubt that most national systems have a more or less marked regional bias, but it cannot be inferred that this is a consequence of the system itself. A guarantee instrument cannot bring about a broader regional diversification of direct investments any more that it can steer investment towards particular countries. The claim that at the same time the existence of country ceilings leads to discrimination once this limit has been reached is no more sustainable than the view that large investments would no longer be covered. These are obviously generalisations based on short-term experiences with the American OPIC and deliberations within the British scheme. In the case of the Federal Republic of Germany there is no evidence of restrictive underwriting practices of the kind alleged against investments in particular regions or for large-scale projects, particularly in the energy and mining sector.

A disadvantage of all national schemes from the point of view of resource allocation is that they restrict insurance cover to their own nationals. This national orientation is quite understandable, particularly if one visualises the situation prevailing when these measures were introduced; it does not pay sufficient regard to the requirement of an integrated world economy marked by increased collaboration between enterprises.

It must be conceded that a multilateral agency does offer some advantages with regard to the insurance of consortium projects. However, this too must be qualified, for apart from the fact that a national scheme could widen its range of business by changing its articles, parallel insurance would also be able to meet the needs of consortium members. Under such an arrangement, the conclusion of contracts by the individual firms with their national insurance agency would probably cause no particular problems but would entail higher administrative cost than multilateral negotiations.

In the event of a loss negotiations would, of course, have to be conducted between the various insurers and the host country, but the administrative effort involved depends to a large degree on the prior agreements with regard to legal safeguards. If investment protection along German lines is available, the fear of drawn-out disputes appears unfounded, even where consortia have several members. On the other hand, if the legal protection afforded by the multilateral agency is meagre and ill-defined, the administrative cost may be much higher. Hence the advantages of a multilateral approach are by no means irresistible; they depend crucially on the configuration of the scheme as a whole, but in par-ticular on the legal arrangements. In this context it should be noted that assignment of the investor's claims to the governing body of the multilateral facility - which is a prerequisite for negotiations with a single party - is not fundamentally in the interest of the host country. This became clear in the negative attitude of the Latin American countries towards the IIIA.[1] However, the capital-exporting countries might also fear diplomatic difficulties and thus not necessarily advocate a multilateral institution.

Besides this disadvantage, which is clearly the only one common to all national insurance and guarantee schemes, there is a further shortcoming due to the multiplicity of

1 The consequences of this attitude will be examined more fully when considering the link between the agency and the World Bank.

these arrangements. The brief comparison of the schemes repeatedly revealed that there can be no talk of identy in the terms offered. This conflicts not only with the allocation objective but also casts doubt upon the economic policy aim of providing equal opportunities for a country's firms engaged in international competition. There is some need for harmonisation and co-ordination here in order to forestall an undesirable terms war and the tendency towards the use of subsidies as a special form of protectionism. The necessary measures in this respect might initially be intensified within the framework of the European Communities, but over the long term they should also be further developed at the OECD level. The fact that a terms war has not yet acquired diplomatic significance is no doubt due to the difficulty in analysing its impact and the greater urgency initially attached to the introduction of schemes.

Improvements in individual details and greater standardisation and co-ordination only take care of the disadvantages for those who already have access to such facilities. The undisputed fact that this form of promotion is unavailable to some industrial countries and practically all the developing countries is not altered by the possible improvements described above.

Given the minor importance of investment on a south-south or south-north basis so far, as evidenced by the modest size of such capital investment,[1] the establishment of national schemes in Third World countries would probably make little

---

1 See S. LALL, The Emergence of Third World Multinationals, Indian Joint Ventures Overseas, in: World Development, Vol. 10, No. 2, Oxford and Frankfurt am Main 1982, pp. 127 ff.; S. LALL, Developing Countries in the International Economy, London and Basingstoke 1981, pp. 24 ff. Lall expresses the view that investment by developing countries among themselves is increasing rapidly. He considers multinational companies of this kind better than the normal type from the point of view of the world economy, although he presents no conclusive evidence to substantiate this claim.

sense on account of the high cost of introducing and imple-
menting an incentive policy such as this, both in terms of
administrative arrangements and expenditure on the additional insurance measures. The burden this would entail would
probably exceed the limited ability of most developing
countries to raise capital and would bear no relationship to
the foreseeable volume of incentives. The developing countries' justified complaint that this incentive mechanism is
not available to them at present has not been removed by the
creation of a few more national schemes in newly industrialised countries.

Finally, the argument that a multilateral guarantee arrangement might first and foremost mobilise investment from OPEC
states ist enlightening but on the whole unconvincing. As
far as these states are concerned, the question arises
whether:

- from the standpoint of their own manufacturing sector
  they are yet in a position to engage in a significant
  volume of direct investment rather than portfolio investment;

- such investment would take place in developing countries;

- their balance-of-payments surpluses are sufficiently du-
  rable for them to make continual large-scale use of a
  multilateral facility.

A critical appraisal of these questions leads to the conclusion that the need for a multilateral scheme is not sign-
ificantly increased even if the interests of the OPEC states
are taken into consideration.

It is also difficult to sustain the argument that re-insurance with private companies is impossible or expensive. The

first point to be made is that as a rule it is not necessary under most national schemes as the state performs this function de facto. The cost ist admittedly rather high, but this is probably due more to the small volume of such business than to particularly high risks caused by regional concentration, as the World Bank assumes. Here too, a problem peculiar to OPIC has obviously been taken to apply to all national guarantee schemes.

On the whole, examination of the two main premisses - the use of foreign direct investment to overcome balance-of-payments problems and the inadequacy of the national investment guarantee schemes - does not prove convincingly that the establishment of a multilateral investment insurance agency would be either necessary in view of the existing problems of sufficient to resolve them. Doubts as to the benefits of the proposed scheme redouble if one looks at certain details of the scheme and the consequences for the parties involved.

Chapter V: ANALYSIS OF IMPORTANT CHARACTERISTICS FROM THE
POINT OF VIEW OF IMPLEMENTATION

The World Bank's criticism of national guarantee schemes
conveys the impression that its suggested solution to the
problem will bring additional advantages for all parties involved, even though its complementary nature is stressed ex-
plicitly. Hence the multilateral facility would have to be
in a position to include and adequately insure both traditional and newer forms of foreign involvement in enterprises
located in developing countries.

§ 10.   *Insurable investment, membership and risks cover*

All that can be ascertained so far from the present draft
outlining the principles of the multilateral guarantee agency is that foreign direct investment is to be safeguarded
against political risks. Using a broad interpretation of the
term, this should comprise both equity participations and
loans equivalent to participations. As the multilateral
facility would probably endeavour to align with the terms
set by national schemes, it is not improbable that the range
of insurable transactions might also include so-called
service contracts, untied loans from non-banks and possibly
licensing agreements.

If this were the case, the multilateral system would simply
mirror the terms of most of the existing national schemes.
The provision of cover for a wider range of transactions
cannot be expected; moreover, it would appear difficult on
technical grounds. This is particularly true of transfers of
know-how that are not laid down in clearly distinguishable
licensing agreements. If they are linked directly with the

export of goods they generally fall within the scope of export credit insurance. Cover under an investment guarantee would seem almost impossible on technical grounds, as the precise loss is likely to be very difficult to assess owing to the problem of defining the insured item. Hence it cannot be inferred that the multilateral guarantee facility is potentially superior as far as the forms of investment are concerned.

Similarly, the multilateral scheme would bring no obvious innovations or extensions in the eligible branches of economic activity. The reference to foreign direct investment suggests that attention will be concentrated chiefly on manufacturing enterprises in the agricultural and industrial sectors, with particular emphasis on energy and mining projects. The coverage of enterprises in the tertiary sector - expecially banks - is unlikely to go further than the national arrangements.

Although the proposal unequivocally defines the scheme's policy-holders and liable member states, the *role of the host countries* is still insufficiently clear. All that is certain is that only investments in developing countries are to be guaranteed and that under the proposals on voting rights these countries will have an assured minimum involvement in all decision-making processes.

However, clarification is required on whether membership of the multilateral scheme will be conferred on all developing countries automatically or should be made conditional on the fulfilment of certain requirements. One possible prerequisite would be an express declaration by the host country that as a matter of principle it would permit investments from capital-exporting members of the multilateral scheme. Consideration might also be given to an assurance that such investments would not suffer discrimination by comparison

112

with projects established under bilateral agreements. In addition, the membership of host countries from the Third World might be made conditional on their endorsements of common *legal arrangements* for the treatment of foreign investment (under the broad definition of this term mentioned above) after the fashion of the German investment promotion treaties or on the ratification of an appropriate common agreement.

Such a design - often described as a "GATT for investment"[1] - would greatly increase the efficiency of a multilateral scheme. It has not been mentioned in the presentation of the proposal up to now, however, thus adding weight to the assumption that it is not regarded as an essential attribute of the scheme.

In fact, membership of a guarantee scheme is inseparable from the question of legal protection. The multilateral facility will fall far short of the standard of certain bilateral schemes of this kind unless there are arrangements binding on all participants.

The enumeration of *types of risks*, which is more detailed than other elements in the proposed scheme, shows that in this respect the multilateral agency is aiming for the level reached by national guarantee arrangements. Relatively comprehensive cover, which might extend to measures equivalent to expropriation, can be assumed by taking a broader interpretation of the formula used hitherto, namely "expropriation, confiscation or *equivalent governmental action or*

---

1 See in this connection P. JUHL, Das Konzept der Investitionsgaran-tiezone, in: Investitionen und politische Risiken in Entwicklungs-ländern, DEG, Materialien 6, Cologne December 1978; P. JUHL, Zur Bewältigung politischer Investitionsrisiken in den Entwicklungslän-dern - Das Konzept einer "Free Investment Area", in: Die Weltwirt-schaft, No. 6, 1976.

*inaction which deprives the insured investor of effective
control over or the benefits of his investments".* [1]

The inclusion of such risks would not, however, be an advantage peculiar to the multilateral scheme, for it is essentially available already under most national arrangements.
The World Bank proposal cannot be judged in this respect
unless the insured events are defined precisely, as the
deprival of effective control can entail different determinants, depending on the system of law.

§ 11. *Financing of the scheme*

The questions of finance relate first to clarification of
the initial endowment and then primarily to the level of
premiums, the "sponsorship" system and subrogation. From the
technical point of view the least problematic appears to be
the question of initial finance to cover administrative
expenses. This can be raised through contributions from
investing countries and/or a payment from the World Bank. [2]
In addition, consideration might also be given to levying a
contribution on the host countries. This is hardly feasible
in practice, however, owing partly to the fact that it does
not occur in national schemes and partly to the adverse
economic situation of the developing countries.

After the initial period premium income should cover administrative expenses. This does not seem unrealistic, especially if the body running the multilateral system can draw
on the national schemes for free preliminary and operational
assistance. Premium income in excess of administrative expenses would be used to create reserves. Linked with this is

1 R82-225, op. cit., p. 13, paragraph 46(a) (underlining by the authors).

2 The World Bank could also provide the funds in the form of loan.
114

the expectation that the agency will be financially self supporting[1] over the long term and will thus be able to meet claims out of premium income.

This calls for not only a wide membership and a correspondingly large portfolio but also an appropriate spread of risks and a certain level of premiums. The World Bank proposal indicates nothing as to the level of premiums, but it may be assumed that it will probably be higher than the rates charged by national schemes owing to the aim to create reserves and to achieve financial independence in the long run. A higher level of premiums will be all the more probable if the agency succeeds in:

- guaranteeing a greater volume of investment in countries which hitherto have not been prominent as host countries (possibly because they imply higher risks);

- re-insuring risks with private underwriters. Such insurance would tend to reduce the scheme's need for reserves over the long term, but would be an additional cost factor.

The threefold function of premiums - to meet administrative expenses, to accumulate reserves and to cover the cost of re-insurance - suggests that the level of premiums will be high and thus not particularly attractive. This undoubtedly conflicts with the objective of assembling as wide a membership as possible and attaining a large portfolio of investment distributed throughout the world.

The fact that losses would be borne jointly by all investing countries until the agency had become self-supporting would,

1 See R82-225, op. cit., pp. 13 f., paragraph 48.

of course, help hold down the level of premiums. This *principle of "sponsorship"* is unprecedented in international relations and unquestionably constitutes one of the cornerstones of the proposed system. For that reason alone it warrants closer examination.

This method of financing losses is a considerable advantage for the multilateral scheme as a whole in that premiums do not have to be calculated to cover costs. The World Bank also sees particular benefit in the fact that the capital-exporting countries will not be called upon to meet claims until insurance has been written for investment sponsored by themselves. This advantage is probably insufficient, however, to outweigh the disadvantages of joint liability, which derive from the fact that in this way not only do they bear the risks of their own commitments but are ultimately also liable for the imponderables of all other investment in all host countries. This is likely to become a problem primarily if a large volume of high-risk investments are accepted for cover owing to the complementary nature of the multilateral scheme.

The capital-exporting countries will find it necessary to set aside additional reserves to cover losses incurred by investors in other countries if the use of public funds is not possible. Apart from the fact that the insurance institution in an individual country would have difficulty calculating the level of reserves required as it would not have full insight into the business potential of the agency, it is hard to imagine that countries would show great willingness to accept liability for risks in countries in which they themselves would have pursued a very cautious underwriting policy. If public funds were to be used, the necessary legal procedures would first have to be established. Here too, it seems doubtful that the state would be prepared to do this.

The appeal of "sponsorship" further reduced by the fact that nations would be liable not only up to the amount of their own investment but possibly in excess of that figure, as liability for a larger proportion of losses is not ruled out where the World Bank considers an investment to be particularly risky.[1] The proposal does not state whether and to what extent countries with less risky investments would then be called upon to pay a smaller proportion.

From the standpoint of national insurers the sponsorship arrangement entails joint liability for a considerable volume of risks that are difficult to calculate. For that reason they might try to be very restrictive in assessing transactions for the multilateral scheme. Furthermore, as they would probably try to insure all less risky investment themselves,[2] this could mean that capital-exporting countries with guarantee schemes of their own would offer the multilateral agency only a small number of transactions.

Hence the proposed arrangement in fact offers clear advantages only for the developing countries. Even though the World Bank stresses that this should not simply transfer the risks of all the members to investors alone,[3] that is precisely the effect produced by the sponsorship system, which might possibly absolve countries that in certain cases are partially responsible for the occurence of the political risk contingency from all obligation to pay compensation. The wording of the World Bank proposal gives the impression that investing countries would be primarily liable to meet claims. That this is only the case if compensation cannot be obtained from the country causing the loss is not stressed, however.

1 See R82-225, op. cit., p. 15, paragraph 57.
2 This applies against the background of the World Bank's not wholly justified criticism of the national schemes.
3 See R82-225, op. cit., p. 17, paragraph 63.

In this connection it again becomes clear how important are legal arrangements to protect investments, even in a multilateral scheme. Further discussion about the creation of a multilateral facility is likely to be meaningful from the point of view of capital-exporting countries only if their obligation to sponsor investment is the exeption rather than the rule.

The question to be asked is why sponsorship must be confined to investing countries. At most, this could be justified on the grounds of the developing countries' low economic capacity. On the other hand, there is something to be said for including host countries in sponsorship. A sensible level of host country participation could imply that the capital-importing countries also form a community that would cover risks arising within their ranks in conjunction with the group of investing countries. Essentially it is a question of developing countries that are not directly involved bearing part of a loss caused by one of their number and for which it should have borne responsibility under international law or accepted agreements but for which it refuses to pay compensation or concedes inadequate amounts. However, it is hardly likely that the country at fault would contribute towards a settlement if it refuses to acknowledge its legal liability.

If the multilateral agency and the host country have concluded an agreement to give investment legal protection, the agency is responsible for all *claims* lodged by the investor or investors in the event of a loss. Further questions arise as to:

- the assessment of subrogation from the viewpoint of investors and host countries;

- the restitution of payments made under the sponsorship arrangements if the host country does nevertheless pay compensation at a later date.

From the purely formal point of view no objections whatever can be raised to the insurer enforcing a claim on behalf of his policy-holder. Problems might possibly arise from the fact that the political reactions of a multilateral body are different to those of a national insurer.

Subrogation appears more problematic from the perspective of the developing countries. The planned link between the World Bank and the guarantee agency apparently causes some to fear that their behaviour towards perhaps only individual foreign investments would have an impact on their entire credit standing with the World Bank, its affiliates and possibly even the International Monetary Fund. This was probably one of the reasons why the Latin American countries in partic-ular registered strong opposition to similar proposals under the IIIA scheme in the past. Their attitude has clearly not changed since then, so that their assent to a new multilat-eral facility will be very difficult to achieve. There might be a stronger possibility if investors themselves concluded a legal protection agreement with the host country that included the necessary ICSID clauses. As the negotiating strength of an individual firm is limited when dealing with a state, such an arrangement would place the investor in a much weaker position than if he were insured under his coun-try's guarantee scheme. Seen in this light, even "parallel insurance" of consortium investments would suit him better than recourse to the multilateral facility.

It might well happen that the host country paid compensation after the sponsorship liabilities had been called. If com-pensation were made to the multilateral agency, it would have to be returned to the sponsors in the due proportions.

It is also conceivable, however, that it would be added to the reserves. This issue still requires clarification.

On the whole, the sponsor arrangement is considerably more complicated to operate that the procedures generally used by national insurance institutions. The extent to which it might be invoked in future is almost impossible for the capital-exporting countries to calculate and might make them very cautious towards the entire multilateral scheme. The governing body would therefore have difficulty winning the number of members needed to reach the desired volume of business. Additional problems arise if claims under the scheme are lodged by an agency closely associated with a multilateral development institution such as the World Bank.

§ 12.   *The link with the World Bank and the existing national guarantee institutions*

A series of arguments can be advanced in favour of the proposed close link between the agency and the World Bank. For example, it is undoubtedly true that the information stored at the Bank on the economic and social situation of member countries and on the assessment of discussions with the governments of individual developing countries helps greatly to improve the understanding of investment terms and the possible risks. In the same way, the exploitation of staff expertise could have a favourable impact on the work of the agency. Both of these factors should permit a reduction in administrative costs, particularly during the initial period, and should also help prevent the growth of an inappropriately large bureaucracy over the long term.

One can also agree with the view that the link with the World Bank would enhance the international standing of the new organisation. The reputation of the World Bank might

120

possibly persuade sceptical industrial countries to participate in the proposed scheme in a way that the unpredictable behaviour of a new institution could not.

Moreover, establishment of the scheme should also be favoured by the fact that the Bank could, if need be, meet at least part of the administrative costs during the initial period. With the Bank's help the legal arrangements that the industrial countries in particular consider necessary to protect investments could be more easily obtained from individual governments or at the multilateral level.

Despite these advantages, there are a number of conflicts of interest that are difficult to resolve. Many developing countries oppose the link between the Bank and the agency because they fear that their investment policies might have adverse repercussions on the Bank's willingness to lend to them. This could also have implications for borrowing from other official and private sources of finance owing to the World Bank's leading role in multilateral development financing. Moreover, as described above, it is also feared that negotiations with the agency over compensation for losses might impair the general reputation of the country, but especially its creditworthiness.

If host countries continue to insist on a strict separation between the insurance of foreign investment and the lending activities of the World Bank, the advantages of an institutional and staff link between the two bodies as set out in the proposal would largely evaporate. The entire organisation would become larger and in any event considerably more costly. Future negotiations would therefore first have to establish whether a more flexible attitude can be achieved among those developing countries that have rejected the link up to now.

The proposed *collaboration between the agency* responsible for the multilateral guarantee scheme and the existing *national institutions* for the insurance of overseas investment raises a number of questions. The least complicated of these is probably the technical matter of assessing insurance applications for the multilateral agency. The majority of the bodies operating in this field in industrial countries have many years' experience and considerable technical expertise, so that they would be able to process applications for multilateral guarantees on the basis of guidelines laid down by the new facility. Some of the newer bodies might be well advised to seek technical assistance from the agency during the initial period.

The possibility touched upon in the World Bank proposal that the national insurance institutions would carry out only initial screening and leave the final assessment to the staff and/or management organs of the agency also seems generally practicable. These questions can most probably be settled, given the national agencies' readiness in principle to co-operate with a multilateral scheme.

By contrast, difficulties are likely to arise on the question of the type and volume of investment to be offered to the multilateral agency. On the assumption that the proposal's criticism of shortcomings in the national insurers have little inducement to hand over a significant volume of business to the multilateral scheme. Provided restrictive underwriting practices caused by regional concentrations or financial constraints on the scale of particular investments do not generally occur and provided at least parallel insurance can be obtained for consortium projects, there is basically no pressing need for a complementary facility. The same applies to the emphasis the World Bank lays on the need for re-insurance with private underwriters, which is of minor importance at best for many national schemes.

Co-insurance might possibly have a part to play in overcoming temporary shortages of capacity. However, it seems on the whole to be better suited to private insurers working in conjunction with a multilateral organisation, as they would be in a better position to align their terms more closely with those of state guarantee schemes.

Provided no serious restrictions develop in underwriting at national level, it would make little sense to divide up business in such a way that particularly risky projects were passed to the multilateral agency, for the view that in the event of a loss national insurers would not be liable for the entire loss but only for the sponsored share proves to be superficial. If several or all national insurers behaved in this way indemnity payments might be higher than if they had written insurance individually owing to their liability for each other's losses under the sponsorship arrangements. Moreover, the problem of the legal protection of investment arises here again. If the legal agreements between the national scheme and a host country were more stringent than the arrangements of the multilateral agency, this would probably also influence the compensation paid by the host country and hence the level of the ultimate loss. The national guarantee would therefore prove economically more advantageous for the investing country.

There is probably also little incentive for firms seeking insurance to turn to the multilateral facility in future rather than to the national institutions as in the past. This can be argued primarily on the grounds that:

- potential technical and administrative difficulties are easier to resolve at national level;[1]

[1] The World Bank is fully aware of this advantage. For that reason it proposes that at least the initial screening be carried out at national level.

- from the subjective viewpoint of the firm, the confidentiality of information on a planned investment appears to
  be safer with an insurance institution in the firm's own
  country than with a multilateral body that is difficult
  to supervise;

- insurance terms as a whole are unlikely to be more favourable than those offered by national insurers and it
  is highly probable that premiums will be higher;

- depending on the final arrangement adopted, firms themselves might have to take more extensive measures to
  obtain legal safeguards for their investments than in the
  case of insurance by a national institution working with
  bilateral investment promotion treaties, as in the case
  of the German scheme.

The World Bank proposal stresses that the membership of a
"relatively small number of capital-exporting and capital-importing countries"[1] would be sufficient to launch the
scheme. However, this can hardly be interpreted to mean that
over the medium and long terms efforts will not be made
greatly to increase the number of members and the portfolio
of investments. Such expansion is necessary on actuarial
grounds and is an important requirement for achieving permanent financial independence without sponsorship. It must
be doubted whether this is possible without a clear demarca-
tion of the respective fields of activity of the existing
institutions and the new facility or allocating certain
types of investment to the new body.

§ 13. *Legal agreements for the protection of investment*

The question of legal protection is one of the key problems
for foreign investment, but in the current World Bank propos-

124

al it receives rather cursory treatment. Effective agreements in this field have a direct influence on the investment climate and are in fact essential if political risks are to be made insurable at all.

In judging the options proposed for the multilateral facility it must be borne in mind that relatively stringent bilateral agreements already exist between capital-exporting and capital-importing countries, such as under the German scheme. Here too the new system must offer at least comparable conditions if it is to be attractive to investors.

In the past, fears were often expressed by industrial countries that legal protection under a multilateral facility would be lower because the most stringent arrangement would not serve as the standard. It is more probable that the highest common denominator would be adopted so that as many host countries as possible could be included. The negotiations in 1979 between the EC and the ACP countries for the Second Lomé Convention showed how difficult it is to attain high standards of legal protection.

In reality, it would be more effective if the multilateral agency negotiated bilateral investment protection agreements with developing countries. It should be made absolutely clear to the developing countries that investors regard such agreements as a *conditio sine qua non*, as a symbol of the host countries' positive attitude towards foreign investment and as proof of their preparedness to abide by a minimum "code of conduct" in the event of a loss; again, intergovernmental and multilateral negotiations are much more successful in making this point.

An all-embracing ideal solution would be to establish a kind of "GATT for foreign investment" and thereby create an investment area with uniform minimum standards in which above

125

all the principles of non-discrimination and most-favoured-nation treatment were applied.[1] Accession to such a multilateral system of legal protection could then be made a condition of membership of the multilateral insurance agency. However, the World Bank proposal does not indicate that the problems of legal protection are to be brought into negotiations on the facility in this way or with the necessary insistence.

1 See P. JUHL, Das Konzept einer Investitionsgarantiezone, op. cit.; Zur Bewältigung politischer Investitionsrisiken in den Entwicklungsländern - Das Konzept einer "Free Investment Area", op. cit.; Die Bedeutung von Investitionsschutzabkommen für Direktinvestitionen und den Technologietransfer in Entwicklungsländern, in: Zeitschrift für betriebswirtschaftliche Forschung, Vol. 33, No. 2, 1981; P.M. GOLD-BERG, C.P. KINDLEBERGER, Toward a GATT for Investment: A Proposal for Supervision of the International Corporation, in: S.P. SETHI, J.N. SETHI (eds.), Multinational Business Operations I. Environmental Aspects of Operating Abroad, Pacific Palisades 1973.

Chapter VI: COMPATIBILITY OF THE MULTILATERAL SCHEME WITH
              THE INTERESTS OF VARIOUS COUNTRY GROUPS

Having examined the requirements underlying the World Bank
proposal and discussed selected problems of implementation,
we shall conclude by investigating the extent to which such
an approach accords with the interests of capital-exporting
and capital-importing countries. In this respect we shall be
looking at both the need for such a tool and its possible
repercussions.

§ 14. *Capital-exporting countries*

At present it cannot be said that national schemes are fundamentally inferior to a multilateral facility. Similarly,
the complaint that certain regions, industries or major
projects are placed at a disadvantage does not appear to
hold true for national schemes as a whole.

Naturally, this does not rule out the possibility that firms
seeking insurance would not give preference to more comprehensive arrangements than those provided by national schemes
if they offered:

- lower costs,

- more extensive coverage of risks,

- higher own payments,

- a lighter administrative burden.

However, these desiderata from the point of view of the individual firm are unlikely to be fulfilled by the World Bank's multilateral facility outlined above. Insofar as the relevant features are mentioned at all and described in sufficient detail, the proposed agency shows a clear tendency to equal the average level of the existing schemes. In some respects, such as premiums or legal protection, the multilateral arrangement seems to entail definite disadvantages in comparison with the schemes run by leading capital-exporting countries.

Against this background, a complementary multilateral guarantee facility will scarcely be in a position to mobilise a substantial and permanent additional flow of capital for direct investment in the Third World. There is therefore little point in detailed consideration of the positive or negative effects the scheme might have on the development and structure of the economies of capital-exporting countries.

One of the main arguments advanced for the creation of a multilateral guarantee facility is that numerous potential capital exporters must allegedly forego overseas investment almost entirely because they have no access to insurance against political risks in developing countries.

Among the *industrial countries* of the Western world, however, only Ireland and Greece[1] have no scheme of this kind. This may place enterprises in these countries at some disadvantage, but the world role of these states as capital exporters is so small owing to the structure and capitalisation of their enterprises that their inclusion in a multi-

---

1 Portugal and South Africa are in the process of establishing overseas investment insurance schemes.

lateral scheme would contribute little to the objectives pursued by means of the World Bank proposal.[1]

The situation is not much different for the *OPEC states* with balance-of-payments surpluses. Since 1973 they have accumulated a considerable volume of capital that is not entirely suitable for direct investment in developing countries. Moreover, it is questionable whether a readiness to undertake capital investments is present in these countries. In this connection it must be pointed out that it would probably be difficult to use the capital surpluses primarily for direct investment, for most oil-producing surplus countries do not at present have the industrial and entrepreneurial potential to carry out such investment on a large scale. Investors will therefore prefer portfolio investments or quasi-participation loans. Up to now this capital has mainly sought investment opportunities with good yields and high security in industrial countries. The reduction of political risks by a multilateral guarantee agency might possibly divert some capital towards developing countries, but only on a limited scale. It should also be remembered that the surpluses are now much less significant than when the World Bank proposal was formulated. Such an instrument would therefore be of only secondary importance in bringing about a lasting increase in co-operation among developing countries themselves.

In spite of this qualification, there can be little doubt that the proposed instrument accords with the interests of the OPEC countries, and their representatives confirmed this during the initial consultations.

---

1 Ireland and Greece are mainly locations for inward investment by companies from other European countries, the United States of America and Japan.

Other developing countries that are industrialising and
already export capital (e.g. some countries in South-East
Asia and Latin America) or are likely to do so owing to
their industrial potential despite their low overall level
of development (e.g. India) have a less strong interest,
however. They seem to be backing regional or national solu-
tions[1] rather than the multilateral scheme. Their cautious
attitude towards the World Bank proposal is probably also
due in part to the fact that these countries will continue
to import a large volume of capital in the form of direct
investment and have little liking for the proposed link
between the World Bank and the insurance agency.

§ 15. *Capital-importing countries*

Bearing in mind the small amount of additional capital that
will be mobilised - primarily from a few OPEC countries - a
complementary multilateral scheme seems to hold relatively
little importance for the capital-importing developing countries. Another reason is the limited suitability of such an
instrument to steer investment towards regions that have
been neglected up to now. Any additional investment that is
generated will probably be concentrated as before in newly
industrialising countries which already have a high purchasing power, in states with potentially large domestic markets
and in areas with mineral deposits that are relatively easy
to extract but difficult to substitute. There is therefore
little reason for the group of least developed countries to
hope to obtain capital and know-how in this way.

---

1 Evidence of this may be seen in the continuation of studies for an
insurance scheme to be run by the Inter-American Development Bank
(IDB) and in the creation of national schemes in India and Korea.

Conclusion: RESULTS OF THE ANALYSIS AND THE PROSPECTS FOR
POSSIBLE ALTERNATIVES

The overall conclusion to be drawn from the analysis is that
the proposal for a multilateral investment insurance agency
has little prospect of implementation in the near future.
This finding can be substantiated mainly on the following
grounds:

- a multilateral guarantee scheme is not a suitable way of
  meeting the developing countries' need for a lasting
  broad additional flow of direct investment. This promotional instrument alone is unlikely to channel resources
  towards host countries that have hitherto played only a
  subsidiary role, if any. This requires a longer-term
  process of successful development that leads to an
  improvement in investment opportunities;

- most of the national investment insurance schemes are
  more effective than the World Bank assumes. The regional
  concentration in various countries, which reflects the
  motives of investors and profitable investment opportunities, is not a disadvantage per se. Provided there are
  no country ceilings, restrictive underwriting practices
  have little effect on either investment in particular
  countries or major projects. Hence the interest of investors and national insurers in a complementary multilateral facility must be regarded as small. The same applies
  to co-insurance;

- all important investing countries now have their own
  overseas investment insurance schemes, which can also cover forms of participation other than the classical direct investment. This considerably narrows the proposed

131

scope for a multilateral agency. Among the capital-exporting countries it is probably only a few members that feel a real need for the creation of such a body. However, it is questionable whether their propensity to invest in developing countries and their investment opportunities justify the establishment of a multilateral facility. It would seem simpler to extend the business activities of the Inter-Arab Guarantee Corporation to include non-Arab host countries;

- premiums charged by a multilateral scheme that must first accumulate the necessary reserves and may also have to bear re-insurance costs are likely to be higher than those of national institutions;

- the system of "sponsorship" financing places high and indeterminable burdens on the national investment insurance schemes;

- investment protection agreements are an indispensable part of an effective multilateral guarantee scheme. At the very least, their importance seems to have been underplayed in the World Bank proposal. Furthermore, there are doubts whether the substance and effects of the agreements meet the standard set in the bilateral investment promotion treaties of the Federal Republic of Germany, for example;

- the planned close link between the insurance agency and the World Bank makes sense from the points of view of administration and cost. However, it is unacceptable to many host countries because of the possible intermingling of traditional World Bank activities and guarantee business.

If these findings are compared with the reasons stated by the World Bank for the abandonment of work on the IIIA in 1973, it can be seen that the problems already existing then have not been resolved in the new proposal. Then as now, the main obstacles to the creation of a multilateral guarantee institution lie in the lack of interest among member countries and in doubts on legal questions and the link with the World Bank. Furthermore, both proposals remain unclear about the final arrangements for financing, voting rights and further technical details.

In view of the minor benefit that the introduction of a multilateral investment guarantee scheme can be expected to produce for the world economy and for development efforts, neither the major capital-exporters nor the capital-importers will be prepared to give the proposal wholehearted and lasting support. It is therefore appropriate to reflect on alternative measures that might be taken to remove or avoid those obstacles and shortcomings in the political risks field that national systems cannot cover or have actually caused.

For example, it cannot be overlooked that in some cases there are quite substantial differences in the terms available. These mainly affect the settlement of claims because of the different approaches to valuation (see Chapter IV, § 9 a.7). The possibility of a terms war cannot be permanently excluded. This would have an adverse effect on the world economy by falsifying profitability differences. Taking a long-term view, there is therefore a *need for standardisation and co-ordination*.

As far as the western industrialised countries are concerned, the OECD and the Berne Union are institutions that could undertake co-ordination and standardisation functions or are already active in this sphere. The examples of India and Ko-

133

rea show that it is not unrealistic to expect further schemes to be set up by newly industrialised countries, although at present the unsolved debt problems constitute an obstacle. As further guarantee schemes are created in NICs, the question of the forum for exchanges of ideas and co-ordination with these national institutions will become more acute. In this respect the World Bank - or its subsidiary the International Finance Corporation (IFC), which has experience in the field of investment - could already prepare the way by giving Third World countries any help they requested to establish guarantee schemes. This could take the form of both expertise and loans.

The countries that already have fully operational guarantee schemes might have a greater interest in standardisation in future if *investment by consortia* really did increase in importance. Harmonisation of the principles for setting terms would greatly ease the formulation of *ad hoc project guarantees.* Such ad hoc collaboration among several national guarantee institutions for particular investment projects is on the whole preferable to a centralised multilateral agency, firstly on account of the saving in administrative expense (lower joint costs) and secondly because of the greater identity of interests and the resultant better adaptation of terms to suit the individual case. The views of host countries can also be taken into consideration in this respect.

The objections to a multilateral investment guarantee scheme also apply in the main to *regional schemes,* so that the latter would not offer a suitable alternative. The same may be said of the establishment of a *multilateral re-insurance agency,* which is beset by the same problems as a multilateral guarantee scheme with regard to the governing body, financing and voting rights. The state agencies responsible for national schemes will show little interest in such re-insurance owing to the uncertain impact on their overall costs. The possibility of re-insurance on a multilateral basis might induce private investment insurers to expand their activities. However, in the event of a loss, they too would then have an interest in assigning to the re-insurer claims against the expropriating country ceded to them by the policy-holder. It must be doubted whether the home country of an expropriated direct investment will be interested in assuming such rights, as there is a danger of political complications.

The most sensible alternative to a multilateral guarantee scheme lies in a *multilateral investment protection agreement as a complement to the ICSID*. Such an agreement, which could be broadened into a "GATT" for direct investment by means of a genuine most-favoured-nation clause, would remove a serious obstacle to the flow of risk capital into developing countries, namely legal uncertainty. Moreover, as mentioned several times above, such an accord would help reduce the costs of national schemes and would thus presumably remove any basis for entertaining proposals for the introduction of a multilateral re-insurance institution.

Future efforts to achieve a "GATT for investment" must, however, take care that the results do not fall short of the standard set by the German investment promotion treaties. As capital importers in the Third World would then still have sufficient scope to channel direct investment according to their own objectives, it should be possible to obtain the necessary international consensus for the benefit of the world economy.

BIBLIOGRAPHY

Books and Essays

Al-Ani, A.
Deutsche Direktinvestitionen in Entwicklungsländern, in: Wirtschaftsdienst, Vol. 49, No. 4, Hamburg 1969

Amin, S.
Underdevelopment and Dependence in Black-Africa - Their Historical Origins and Contemporary Forms, in: Social and Economic Studies, Vol. 22, No. 2, 1973

Beyfuß, J.
Exportversicherung und Exportfinanzierung. Ein internationaler Vergleich, Beiträge zur Wirtschafts- und Sozialpolitik, Institut der deutschen Wirtschaft, 115, Cologne 1983

Brandt, W. et al.
North-South, a Programme for Survival: Report of the Independent Commission on International Development Issues, London 1980

Clausen, A.W.
Third World Debt and Global Recovery. The 1983 Jodidi Lecture at the Centre for International Affairs, Harvard University., Boston/Mass., February 24, 1983

Dickie, R.B.
An Examination of Equity Sharing Policies: What Causes Them to Fail - and to Succeed, in: Columbia Journal of World Business, Vol. 16, No. 2 1981

Domitra, M.
Krise in der Rohstoffversorgung der westlichen Welt? Expertengespräch in Washington am 11. und 12. Dezember 1980, 1981

Dunning, J.H.
The Determinants of International Production, in: Oxford Economic Papers, New Series, Vol. 25, New Jersey 1973

Egli, A.
Die volkswirtschaftliche Bedeutung des Technologietransfers nach Entwicklungsländern, Birsfelden 1974

Fels, G.
Die Textilindustrie und das Theorem der komparativen
Kosten - eine "Erwiderung", Kieler Diskussionsbeiträ-
ge, No. 27, Kiel January 1973

Gerber, S.
Risikoanalyse und Risikopolitik bei direkten deutschen
Auslandsinvestitionen von mittelständischen Unterneh-
mungen in Entwicklungeländern, Frankfurt am Main 1982

Giersch, H. (ed.)
Reshaping the World Economic Order, Symposium 1976,
Tübingen 1977

Giesel, F.
Kapitalstrukturen internationaler Unternehmungen,
Gießener Schriftenreihe zur Internationalen Unterneh-
mung, Vol. 1, Gießen 1982

Gilman, M.G.
The Financing of Foreign Direct Investment: A Case
Study of the Determinants of Capital Flow in Multina-
tional Enterprises, London 1981

Goldberg, P.M.; Kindleberger C.P.
Toward a GATT for Investment: A Proposal for Supervi-
sion of the International Corporation, in: Sethi, S.P.;
Sethi, J.N. (eds.), Multinational Business Operations
I. Environmental Aspects of Operating Abroad, Pacific
Palisades 1973

Grosse, R.E.
Foreign Investment Codes and the Location of Direct
Investment, New York 1980

Gutowski, A.; Holthus, M.
Limits to International Indebtedness, in: Donald J.
Fair (ed.), International Lending in a Fragile World
Economy, The Hague 1983

Halbach, A.-J.; Osterkamp, R.; Riedel, J.
Die Investitionspolitik der Entwicklungsländer und
deren Auswirkungen auf das Investitionsverhalten deutscher Unternehmen, Munich and London 1982

Hallén, L.
International Industrial Purchasing Channels, Interaction and Governance Structures, Uppsala 1982

Haner, F.T.
Rating Investments Abroad,   in: Business Horizons,
April 1979

Haubold, D.
Direktinvestitionen und Zahlungsbilanz, Hamburg 1972

Helmstetter, E.
Die Chancen der Textil- und Bekleidungsindustrie in
hochentwickelten Ländern - Ein empirischer Beitrag zu
kontroversen Fragen der Standortsuche beider Industriezweige, Kieler Diskussionsbeiträge No. 34, Kiel, December 1972

Holthus, M.
Verschuldung und Verschuldungsfähigkeit von Entwicklungsländern, in: Hamburger Jahrbuch für Wirtschafts-
und Gesellschaftspolitik, Vol. 26, Tübingen 1981

Jacobi, von, I.
Direktinvestitionen und Export, Hamburg 1972

Jägeler, F.J.; Wagner, W.; Wilhelm, W.
Radar für Auslandsrisiken, in: Managermagazin, No. 1,
Hamburg 1981

Jüttner, H.
Förderung und Schutz deutscher Direktinvestitionen in
Entwicklungsländern unter besonderer Berücksichtigung
der Wirksamkeit von Investitionsförderungsverträgen,
Internationale Kooperation, Aachener Studien zur internationalen technisch-wirtschaftlichen Zusammenarbeit, Vol. 15, Baden-Baden 1975

Juhl, P.
Das Konzept einer Investitionsgarantiezone, in:
Investitionen und politische Risiken in Entwicklungs-
ländern, DEG, Materialien 6, Cologne, December 1978

Die Bedeutung von Investitionsschutzabkommen für Direktinvestitionen und den Technologietransfer in Entwicklungsländern, in: Zeitschrift für betriebswirtschaftliche Forschung Vol. 33, No. 2, 1981

Zur Bewältigung politischer Investitionsrisiken in den
Entwicklungsländern - Das Konzept einer "Free Investment Area", in: Die Weltwirtschaft, No. 1, 1976

Jungnickel, R.; Koopmann, G.; Matthies, K.; Sutter, R.;
Holthus, M. (eds.)
Die deutschen multinationalen Unternehmen, Frankfurt am
Main 1974

Kayser, G.; Kitterer, B.H.-J.; Naujoks, W.; Schwarting,
U.; Ullrich, K.V.
Investieren im Ausland. Was deutsche Unternehmen drau-
ßen erwartet, Bonn (no date)

Kebschull, D.
Alternativen internationaler Entwicklungsfinanzierung,
in: Schäfer, H.-B., Gefährdete Weltfinanzen, Bonn
1980

Die Wirkungen von Auslandsinvestitionen auf das Beschäftigungsniveau, in: Krise und Reform der Industriegesellschaft, Vol. 2, Frankfurt am Main 1976

Exportförderung als Problem nationaler Außenhandelspolitik, in: Gegenwartskunde - Zeitschrift für Gesellschaft, Wirtschaft, Politik und Bildung, Vol. 16, No.
1, 1976

Motive für deutsche Direktinvestitionen in Entwicklungsländern, in: Probleme der Arbeitsteilung zwischen Industrie- und Entwicklungsländern. Bericht über
den wissenschaftlichen Teil der 35. Mitgliederversamm-
lung der Arbeitsgemeinschaft deutscher wirtschaftswis-
senschaftlicher Institute e.V. in Bad Godesberg am 4.
und 5. Mai 1972, Berlin 1972

Motive, Maßnahmen und Auswirkungen staatlicher Exportförderungspolitik - Das Beispiel Italiens, in: Jahrbuch für Sozialwissenschaft, Vol. 20, No. 2, 1969

Kebschull, D.
Nach Energiekrise - Rohstoffkrise? Probleme der Sicherung unserer Rohstoffbasis, Berlin 1981

Neue Gestaltungsformen und Perspektiven der öffentli-
chen Entwicklungshilfe, in: Simonis U.E. (Ed.),
Entwicklungsländer in der Finanzkrise - Probleme und
Perspektiven, Schriften des Vereins für Socialpolitik,
N.F. Band 136, Berlin 1983 (to be published shortly)

Some remarks on Proposals for Economic Recovery in
Developing Countries, Conference Room Paper No. 7, High
Level Expert Group Meetings Preparatory to the Fourth
General Conference of UNIDO, Lima/Peru, 18-22 April
1983

Worldwide Export Promotion Requires New Concepts, in:
Intereconomics, No. 7, 1966

Zur Anbieterposition der Entwicklungsländer, in: D.
Kebschull (ed.), Rohstoff- und Entwicklungspolitik.
Wissenschaftliche Schriftenreihe des Bundesministeriums
für wirtschaftliche Zusammenarbeit, Vol. 28, Stuttgart
1974

Kebschull, D. et a.
Industrialisierung im Nord-Süd-Dialog - Vorschläge zur
dritten Generalkonferenz von UNIDO und Bewertung des
Verlaufs, in: Forschungsberichte des Bundesministe-
riums für wirtschaftliche Zusammenarbeit, Munich,
Cologne and London 1980

et al., Wirkungen von Privatinvestitionen in Entwicklungsländern, Baden-Baden 1980

Künne, W., Menck, K.W., Das Integrierte Rohstoffprogramm, Hamburg 1977

Mayer, O.G., Deutsche Investitionen in Indonesien,
Hamburg 1974

Kobrin, S.J.
Political Assessment by International Firms, in:
Journal of Policy Modelling, Vol. 3, No. 1, 1981

Krägenau, H.
Internationale Direktinvestitionen, Ergänzungsband
1978/79, Hamburg 1979

Internationale Direktinvestitionen, Ergänzungsband
1982, Hamburg 1982

141

Lall, S.
Developing Countries in the International Economy, London and Basingstoke 1981

The Emergency of Third World Multinationals, Indian Joint Ventures Overseas, in: World Development, Vol. 10, No. 2, Oxford and Frankfurt am Main 1979

Menck, K.W.
Möglichkeiten steuerlicher Förderung von Investitionen in Entwicklungsländern, in: Staatsfinanzierung im Wandel. Verhandlungen auf der Jahrestagung des Vereins für Socialpolitik, Gesellschaft für Wirtschafts- und Sozialwissenschaften in Köln 1982, Berlin 1983 (to be published shortly)

in collaboration with Schwarz, R.E., Technologietransfer in Entwicklungsländer - Der Beitrag deutscher Unternehmen, Hamburg 1981

Micallef, J.V.
Political Risk Assessment, in: Columbia Journal of World Business, Vol. 16, No. 2, 1981

Michalski, W. (ed.)
HWWA-Studien zur Exportförderung, Italien (D. Kebschull), Hamburg 1968

Morton, K.; Tulloch, P.
Trade and Developing Countries, London 1977

Patzina, R.
Rechtlicher Schutz ausländischer Privatinvestitionen gegen Enteignungsrisiken in Entwicklungsländern, Heidelberg and Hamburg 1981

Pirrung, J.
Das Weltbankübereinkommen für Investitionsstreitigkeiten vom 18. März 1965, in: Die Aktiengesellschaft, Vol. 17, 1972

Pollak, C.
Neue Formen internationaler Unternehmenszusammenarbeit ohne Kapitalbeteiligung, Munich, Cologne and London 1982

Prast, W.G.; Lax, H.L.
    Political Risk as a Variable in TNC Decision-Making,
    in: Natural Resources Forum, Vol. 6, No. 2, 1982

Root, F.R.
    Independence and Adaptation: Response Strategies of
    U.S.-Based Multinational Corporations to a Restrictive
    Public Policy World, in: K.P. Sauvant, F.G. Lavipour
    (eds.), Controlling Multinational Enterprises. Prob-
    lems, Strategies, Counterstrategies, Frankfurt am Main
    1976

Rummel, P.J.; Heenan, D.A.
    Wie die Multis politische Risiken analysieren, in:
    Havard Manager 1980, No. III, 1980

Scharrer, H.E. (ed.)
    Förderung privater Direktinvestitionen. Eine Untersu-
    chung der Maßnahmen bedeutender Industrieländer, Ham-
    burg 1972

Schmidt, A. (ed.)
    Strategien gegen Unterentwicklung - Zwischen Weltmarkt
    und Eigenständigkeit, Frankfurt am Main and New York
    1976

Schwamm, H.
    The OECD Guidelines for Multinational Enterprises, in:
    Journal of World Trade Law, Vol. 12, 1978

Seibert, K.
    Joint Ventures als strategisches Instrument im interna-
    tionalen Marketing, Vertriebswirtschaftliche Abhandlun-
    gen, No. 23, Berlin 1981

Servan-Schreiber, J.J.
    The American Challenge, London 1968

Sunkel, O.
    National Development and External Dependence in Latin
    America, in: Journal of Development Studies, Vol. 6,
    No. 1, 1969/70

Torre, de la, J.R.
Exports of Manufactured Goods from Developing Countries: Marketing Factors and the Role of Foreign Enterprise, in: Journal of International Business Studies, Vol. 2, No. 1, 1971

Wagenhöfer, E.
Unsere internationalen Währungsbeziehungen - Grundlagen, Probleme - Entwicklungen, Bonn 1976

Other Publications

Bundesministerium für wirtschaftliche Zusammenarbeit
Deutsche Unternehmen in Entwicklungsländern - ein Handbuch für Lieferungen, Leistungen, Investitionen, 2nd edition, Bonn, May 1982

Club de Dakar
Proposal by the Club de Dakar for the Establishment of an International Guarantee Fund

Deutsche Bundesbank
Die Kapitalverflechtung der Unternehmen mit dem Ausland, in: Monatsberichte der Deutschen Bundesbank, Vol. 33, No. 10, 1981

European Communities
Communication from the Commission to the Council on the need for Community action to encourage European investment in developing countries and guidelines for such action, COM(78)23, Brussels 30th January 1978

Report from the Commission to the Council: Investment promotion and protection clauses in agreements between the community and various categories of developing countries: achievements to date and guidelines for joint action COM(80)204, Brussels 8th May 1980

Friedrich-Ebert-Stiftung
Probleme der Rohstoffsicherung - Expertengespräch in Bonn, 26. und 27. Juni 1980, Kurzfassung der wesentlichen Ergebnisse, 1980

144

IBRD,   International Bank für Reconstruction and Development
        International Investment Insurance Agency, Washington
        D.C., April 16, 1973

        Multilateral   Investment   Insurance,   A   Staff   Report,
        Washington D.C., March 1962

        Multilateral Investment Insurance Agency, R82-225, Juli
        14, Washington D.C., 1982 (referred to as R82-225)

        Multilateral Investment Insurance Agency,   Staff Stud-
        ies, Washington D.C., Juni 1983

        World Development Report, Washington D.C., 1977

        World Development Report, Washington D.C., 1982

International Centre for the Settlement of Investment Disputes, ICSID
        Regulations and Rules, 1968

International Monetary Fund
        Balance of Payments Manual, Washington D.C., 1977

ITE,   Institut zur Erforschung technologischer Entwicklungslinien
        Die   Investitionspolitik   der   NE-Bergbaugesellschaften
        und ihre Auswirkungen auf die Rohstoffversorgung der
        Bundesrepublik Deutschland, Hamburg 1978

OECD,   Organisation for Economic Co-operation and Development
        International Investment and Multinational Enterprises,
        Investment Incentives and Disincentives and the Inter-
        national Investment Process, Paris 1983

        Investing in Developing Countries, New edition adapted
        in August 1972, Paris 1972

        Investing in Developing Countries, Third edition June
        1975, Paris 1975

        Investing   in   Developing   Countries,   Fourth   Revised
        Edition, Paris 1978

        Investing in Developing Countries, Fifth Edition, Paris
        1983

Overseas Private Investment Corporation
A Critical Analysis Prepared for the Committee on Foreign Affairs by the Foreign Affairs Division, Congressional Research Service, Library of Congress, September 4, Washington D.D., 1973

Sachverständigenkommission "Exportförderung Baden-Württemberg" - EFK
Schlußbericht, Stuttgart 1982

Treuarbeit Aktiengesellschaft
Allgemeine Bedingungen für die Übernahme von Garantien für Kapitalanlagen im Ausland, Juli 1978

UNCTAD, United Nations Conference on Trade and Development
Bulletin, No. 192, April 1983

UNIDO, United Nations Industrial Development Organization
Industry 2000, New Perspectives, Third General Conference of UNIDO, New Delhi, 21 January - 8 February 1980, Vienna, September 1979

Joint Study on International Industrial Co-operation, Vienna, May 1979

Wissenschaftlicher Beirat beim Bundesministerium für wirtschaftliche Zusammenarbeit
Stellungnahme zur Auslandsverschuldung der Entwicklungsländer, in: Entwicklungspolitik, BMZ - Aktuell, Bonn, April 1983

Stellungnahme zu den Vorschlägen des zweiten Brandt-Berichts, in: Entwicklungspolitik, BMZ - Aktuell, Bonn, April 1983

No author
Charter of Economic Rights and Duties of States, 12th December 1974, adopted by the 29th General Assembly of the United Nations

A conversation with Mr. Clausen, in: Finance and Development, Vol. 19, No. 4, 1982

Schweden bleibt bei hoher Entwicklungshilfe, in: Frankfurter Allgemeine Zeitung, No. 9 of 12.1.1982

Schweden, Entwicklungshilfe von 1 % des BIP vorgesehen, in: Nachrichten für Außenhandel No. 21 of 30.1.1981

Steuerliche Entwicklungshilfe läuft aus, in: Nachrichten für Außenhandel of 15.9.1981

For Product Safety Concerns and Information please contact our EU representative GPSR@taylorandfrancis.com Taylor & Francis Verlag GmbH, Kaufingerstraße 24, 80331 München, Germany

Printed and bound by CPI Group (UK) Ltd, Croydon, CR0 4YY

01/05/2025
01858403-0001